Substance Abuse Assessment, Interventions and Treatment

COGNITIVE-BEHAVIOURAL INDICATORS OF SUBSTANCE ABUSE

SUBSTANCE ABUSE ASSESSMENT, INTERVENTIONS AND TREATMENT

Preventing and Reducing Underage Drinking
Nathaniel P. Marquis (Editor)
2009. 978-1-60692-588-1

Men and Addictions: New Research
Lyman J. Katlin (Author)
2009. 978-1-60692-098-5

Social Drinking: Uses, Abuses and Psychological Factors
Katherine T. Everly and Eva M. Cosell (Editors)
2009. 978-1-60876-219-4

Cognitive-Behavioural Indicators of Substance Abuse
Samuel Pombo, Filipe Barbosa, Marco Torrado, Nuno Félix da Costa (Authors)
2010. 978-1-61668-416-7

Cognitive-Behavioural Indicators of Substance Abuse
Samuel Pombo, Filipe Barbosa, Marco Torrado and Nuno Félix da Costa (Authors)
2010. 978-1-61668-831-8

Substance Abuse Assessment, Interventions and Treatment

Cognitive-Behavioural Indicators of Substance Abuse

Samuel Pombo, Filipe Barbosa,
Marco Torrado
and Nuno Félix da Costa

Nova Science Publishers, Inc.
New York

For permission to use material from this book please contact us:
Telephone 631-231-7269; Fax 631-231-8175
Web Site: http://www.novapublishers.com

LIBRARY OF CONGRESS CATALOGING-IN-PUBLICATION DATA

Cognitive-behavioural indicators of substance abuse / Samuel Pombo ... [et al.].
p. cm.
Includes index.
ISBN 978-1-61668-416-7 (softcover)
1. Substance abuse--Psychological aspects. 2. Substance abuse--Treatment.
I. Pombo, Samuel.
HV4998.C634 2010
616.86--dc22

2010012185

ISBN: 978-1-61668-416-7

Published by Nova Science Publishers, Inc. ✢ New York

CONTENTS

For permission to use material from this book please contact us:
Telephone 631-231-7269; Fax 631-231-8175
Web Site: http://www.novapublishers.com

LIBRARY OF CONGRESS CATALOGING-IN-PUBLICATION DATA
Cognitive-behavioural indicators of substance abuse / Samuel Pombo ... [et al.].
p. cm.
Includes index.
ISBN 978-1-61668-416-7 (softcover)
1. Substance abuse--Psychological aspects. 2. Substance abuse--Treatment. I. Pombo, Samuel.
HV4998.C634 2010
616.86--dc22

2010012185

ISBN: 978-1-61668-416-7

Published by Nova Science Publishers, Inc. ✢ New York

PREFACE

Problems related to substance use, abuse and dependence are a major concern on societies today, persisting to require considerable attention from the community. For decades studies have been showing that drug consumption represents a main risk factor for physical, social and mental health problems. Unfortunately, reality shows that in many cultures and fractions of population, heavy substance use is the norm. This new book examines the cognitive-behavioral indicators of substance abuse and various corresponding treatment techniques.

Chapter 1

1. INTRODUCTION

Problems related to substance use, abuse and dependence are a major concern on societies today, persisting to require considerable attention from the community. For decades studies have been showing that drug consumption represents a main risk factor for physical, social and mental health problems. Unfortunately, reality shows us that in many cultures and fractions of population, heavy substance use is the norm.

Through the years, the study of addictions has been incredibly attractive across quite a lot of disciplines, including genetics, pharmacology, psychiatry, cognitive, behavioral, social sciences, clinical psychology and also politics. Simple and commonly, addictions could be defined as the continuous use of mood altering drugs (e.g., heroin, cocaine, alcohol) or behaviors (e.g., gambling, compulsive sexual behaviors) despite negative consequences (addiction related problems).

At the present time, scientific pre-clinical and clinical research identifies and certificate dependency as a brain disease, which develops through a complex interplay between environmental and biologic/genetic factors. This evidently means that, in our time, to produce a robust scientific knowledge about addictions, we need to understand the interacting effects of multiple psychobiological variables involved in mechanisms as tolerance, craving, anxiety, executive function and reward.

Numerous studies have shown that the concomitant use of several substances occurs frequently and that both environmental and genetic factors contribute to the overlap between these behaviors. This interaction between multiple substances or addictions may play a functional role in the social and clinical picture of the substance dependent. Sometimes, the use of one addictive substance may lead to the excessive use of another (e.g., alcohol consumption may lead to cocaine use) and frequently the synergic effect of two substances may show the way for another addiction (e.g., alcohol and cannabis may possibly lead to cocaine use). The recognition of these high rates of comorbidity between substance use disorders is vital to mental heath clinicians be able to precisely assess and treat this intricate phenotype of polysubstance abuse individuals.

Chapter 2

2. Polydrug Use: A Brain Cocktail Effect

Abstract

The concomitant use of psychoactive substances is, to a great extent, a widespread reality in research, clinical practice and community. At the present time, patients come to treatment with a much more complex profile of drug use. For instance, patients could be dependent of one drug, abuse one or two, and used occasionally several others. This pattern of use could confound seriously clinical interventions and research trials. In this chapter we will focus on polydrug use patterns, mainly, the concurrent use of opiates and alcohol. Many studies showed that alcohol consumption disturbs heroin addiction rehabilitation, however, heroin users often drink alcohol, and many, drink too much and too often. Could the alcohol consumption in this particular population represent a "minor problem" when compared with a "major heroin problem"? All these interactions will be discussed, especially, the relationship between alcohol use and opiate maintenance treatments.

Keywords: polydrug use, opiate maintenance, alcohol use, treatments.

Being drug and polydrug consumption such a pressing issue in societies, the production of knowledge became an urgent matter since the end of the last century. Based on surveys conducted among the general population and specific groups, data collected in rehabilitation centers have revealed certain trends such as, for instance, that cannabis use mainly occurs during adolescence and young adulthood, that ecstasy can be associated with certain lifestyles and leisure activities, and that heroin use frequently results in marginalization and major health problems. All these approaches have improved understandings of the diversity of drug use patterns and of drug user profiles, suggesting better frameworks for preparation and evaluation of the drug-related interventions targeting populations with frequently very different constraints and needs (EMCDDA, 2009). Nevertheless, the understanding of multiple substance use and the analysis of overlaps between different drug-using populations have been more restricted. This has become particularly clear in last decades with an increasing range of available substances that has resulted in additional potential drug combinations, making more apparent the limitations of substance-specific approaches to understanding drug use patterns and trends.

Polydrug use is a pattern that has been observed in many drug users populations and involves a wide variations in users and patterns of use (for example, from sporadic cannabis use to the daily use of heroin combined with alcohol or cocaine). So, it is quite impossible to arrive at a single definition of polydrug use despite it would be necessary to develop standardized measures.

There are many rationales for integrating different drugs during a single consumption event. When are taken together drugs can have cumulative or complementary effects, so they increase the overall psychoactive experience. In a similar way, offsetting the negative effects of a drug can be another reason to take an additional substance. The continuous use of several substances in a certain period of time might be related with a need to replace one drug by another, alongside with price variations, availability, legality or fashion (Boys et al., 1999). It could also reflect the use of separate drugs in different contexts, or simply reflect regular multi-substance use related with drug dependence. Overall, the types of psychoactive substances that are used in combination depends of many factors such as the personal preferences, local availability, local prescribing medical practices (Gossop et al., 1998). Polydrug use may also reflect the availability of drugs and patterns of consumption in specific contexts (Ives and Ghelani, 2006).

According to EMCDDA literature there have been identified three main profiles among clients entering treatment by consumption of various drugs, the heroin and cocaine (including crack-cocaine), the cocaine and cannabis or alcohol, and finally cannabis and alcohol. The first group is the most numerous and includes marginalized heroin users who also use other substances. The second group, often starts the treatment by judicial system or by pressure from social network and family and mostly consisting of males and well integrated socially. The third group - cannabis and alcohol – is often composed by people living with their family and socially well integrated.

The use of psychoactive substances in early ages is of concern as the brain and other organs are still developing during adolescence, and exposure to toxic substances may cause damage with bad consequences that might only appear in adulthood. Early initiation during adolescence has been linked with higher probability of drug use later in life and greater complications in ceasing drug use (Von Sydow et al., 2002). As we well-known, some addicts initiate their drug consumption early in adolescence, probably due to their curiosity about drugs. At the adolescence, social-functioning is not matured and consciousness for responsibility to family/society is not strong. They lack self-control, judgment, and critical thinking ability. Their behaviors are often driven by instinct and curiosity, and they often hardly consider the consequence of their actions. Because of deficient knowledge of drug harm, some adolescents treat drug consumption as a novel and exciting matters such as a car race or an activity such as mountain-climbing (Yan et al., 2008).

There are evidences that almost all substances affect the neuropsychological domains of attention, memory and learning, spatial abilities and executive functioning. It is also known that their action generally affects the inhibitory control, working memory and decision-making (Yucel et al., 2007). Colzato et al. (2009) studied a recreational cocaine polydrug users group in order to appraise impairments in cognitive flexibility and working memory. The findings suggest that recreational use of cocaine in a polydrug use context selectively impairs cognitive flexibility but not the maintenance of information in working memory, although with negative repercussions for daily life activities in face to this inability to adjust behavior rapidly and flexibly.

The most recent data collected in 22 European countries, resulting from the European Project for Study of Alcohol and Other Drug Use Among Students (ESPAD) of 2003, emphasizes that polydrug use among adolescents (the use of at least two different psychoactive substances at a young age) could be considered an indicator for early initiation. The use of illicit substances that are uncommon at this age could also reflect higher levels of risk behaviors, social exclusion or deviance among adolescents (EMCDDA, 2009). In this study, a little over 20% of students aged 15-16 years mentioned the consumption alcohol and tobacco in the previous month; 6% reported cannabis use, as well as alcohol and tobacco, and 1% said they consume this group of substances and an additional illegal drugs (heroin, ecstasy, cocaine, amphetamines or LSD). It has also been showed that cannabis users tended more to the use of other illicit drugs than the school population aged 15-16 years in general, which is particularly perceptible in countries with low prevalence of drug use, where cannabis use was also associated with family neglect, lack of parental control and truancy.

Among young adults of nine countries it was found that those who consume alcohol in large quantities are more likely to have consumed cannabis or used cocaine during the previous year than the general population (EMCDDA, 2009). These results are analogous with those obtained in a north-american recent study which pointed out that college students with heavy drinking practices appear to experiment with a wider number of illicit drugs than do moderate drinkers; and moderate drinkers appear to experiment more than light drinkers (O'Grady et al., 2008).

Polydrug use often takes place in the context of recreational activities, with population surveys confirming that drug use is associated with visiting bars and nightclubs. A study conducted in 2006 among a sample of 1383 young people in nightlife settings in nine European cities found that the frequent use of individual drugs varies between cities and appears to reflect the prevalence levels among the general population and the availability of the substances. Tobacco, alcohol and cannabis were overall the substances most commonly used on a regular basis (five or more days a week); less than 1 % of respondents reported regular use of other substances. However, the study identified the existence of a very small group of drug users who consumed drugs in an extremely intensive manner. It also found that concomitant alcohol use was common, with 34 % of those interviewed reported having been drunk more than twice during the four weeks before the interview. Drunkenness is likely to increase the risk of making ill-considered decisions about drug taking and was more frequently reported by males than females: 42 % and 27 % respectively (European Commission, 2007).

Two recently conducted studies in recreational settings were reported by Belgium. The first one, surveyed over 2,000 people in three clubs during different events held in 2003, 2005 and 2007. The study found that almost half of those who reported the use of an illicit drug during the last year stated that they regularly combined alcohol and an illicit drug, and one in four drug users commonly combined different illicit drugs. Cannabis and cocaine were used both before and after going out. The second study, in the French Community in 2007, surveyed almost 2500 individuals during music festivals and found that 68 % of respondents used at least one psychoactive substance during such an event (tobacco not included). Some 38 % used only one drug, 18 % used two substances and 12 % used three or more during the event. Among those people who had used alcohol or drugs during the event (*n* = 1 649), the most general combination was alcohol and cannabis. Ecstasy users took an average of three other products (*n* = 165) and cocaine users an average of four other products (*n* = 86).

In the context of recreational drug taking, polydrug use can be time-limited and linked to a specific social situation or location. Evidence suggests that during short holiday periods and weekends, young people are particularly predisposed to indulge in drug-related activities that put them at some kind of risk, which highlights the need for specifically targeted prevention and harm-reduction responses that encompasses the different settings in which polydrug use occurs (Bellis et al., 2003).

When Alcohol Meets Opiates: Alcohol Abuse in Heroin Users

Polydrug use has been reported among substance abusers from treatment and community samples (Martin et al., 1996; Hubbard et al., 1997; Gossop et al., 2002a; Leri et al., 2003; Flannery et al., 2004; Booth et al., 2006; Malcolm et al., 2006; Byqvist, 2006; Darke et al., 2007). Certainly, the use of multiple substances might cause difficulties in the assessment and understanding of addiction (Gossop, 2001). For example, focusing on a single primary substance use possibly will obscure the overall picture of substance use behavior if a concomitant substantial polydrug use exists. In the same way, studies also suggest that multiple dependencies may interfere to successful treatment interventions (Downey et al., 2000; Bovasso and Cacciola, 2003; Williamson et al., 2006). Results from a 33-year follow-up study of 581 heroin addicts indicates that heavy alcohol use was associated with negative outcomes such as more frequent illicit drug use (Hser et al., 2001).

Empirical literature supports the clinical and treatment complications of polydrug use in terms of greater psychopathology (Beswick et al., 2001; Sumnall et al., 2004; Booth et al., 2006; Malcolm et al., 2006; Medina and Shear, 2007); higher levels of health risk behaviors (Patterson et al., 2005); and difficulties in engaging in treatment (John et al., 2001).

Heroin users often drink alcohol excessively (Almog et al., 1993; Backmund et al., 2003). Curiously, while this behavior often causes serious health costs (Gossop et al., 2002b), limited epidemiological data is available. In many cases, it seems that an alcohol problem represents a “minor charge” in a maintenance treatment of a major heroin problem. This "cognitive blindness" related to alcohol abuse in opioid addicts appears to be generalized also to these families, and certainly it could be more concerning if this process also took place in substance abuse therapists.

Approximately 20–50% of methadone maintained therapy (MMT) patients have alcohol-related problems (Rittmannsberger et al., 2000; Hillebrand et al., 2001; Backmund et al., 2003; Dobler-Mikola et al., 2005; Senbanjo et al., 2006; Stenbacka et al., 2007). Variations in prevalence are likely since different definitions of problematic alcohol use are employed and populations studied are heterogeneous (Ottomanelli, 1999; Srivastava et al., 2008). In addition, Ottomanelli (1999) states that "in order to evaluate the extent of alcohol abuse by methadone patients, it is essential to review the prevalence of alcohol abuse in the general population in order to have a comparison base". According to the author, the range for alcohol-abusing methadone patients does not appear to be substantially different from the range rates of "heavier drinkers" in the general population.

Studies demonstrate that preadmission levels of substance use (which includes alcohol) in treatments were predictive of post-admission levels of use (Hunt et al., 1986; Kaufman, 1982), with particular attention to alcohol. A larger history of heroin abuse and its pre-MMT daily consumption predicted additional chronic alcohol use during MMT (Dobler-Mikola et al., 2005). Fairbank et al., (1993) compared the consumption of six substances (cocaine, amphetamines, illegal methadone, marijuana, and chronic alcohol use) in methadone patients' in the 1 year prior to admission with the use of these substances at 1-year follow-up. The results showed decreased substance use in the follow-up year, except for alcohol use, which remained stable during the preadmission and follow-up years.

While contradictory literature exists saying that MMT reduces alcohol use by offering a means of stabilization (Maremmani et al., 2007) or leads to an increase in alcohol use during treatment (Srivastava et al., 2008) and upon discontinuation of treatment (Maremmani et al., 2007), a positive association has been found between alcohol use and relapse into illicit drugs (Stenbacka et al., 2007).

Some studies emphasize that alcohol dependence can deteriorate the outcome of methadone treatment (Ottomanelli, 1999; Gossop et al., 2006) and it's associated with increased psychiatric symptoms (Westreich, 2005). Moreover, alcohol use appears to be associated with more illicit drug use, higher rates of drop-out and higher mortality rates (Joseph and Appel, 1985; Zador and Sunjic, 2000; Hillebrand et al., 2001; Teplin et al., 2007).

Patients who are dependent both on illicit drugs and alcohol may have a poorer treatment outcome than patients without alcohol problems, that is, cause involuntary discharge from treatment (Kreek, 1978; Caputo et al., 2000).

MMT patients often experience mood changes, anxiety and personality disorders, and multiple substance use disorders which are frequently exacerbated by alcohol use (Westreich, 2005). Excessive alcohol consumption among MMT patients has been associated with quality of life impairments (Senbanjo et al., 2006), with MMT program non-completion and are more likely to engage in unprotected sex (Arasteh et al., 2008).

Several studies have shown that a greater percentage of MMT males than females abuse alcohol (Backmund et al., 2003; Stenbacka et al., 2007). It has been shown that methadone-using patients who drink excessively are at a significantly greater risk of getting cirrhosis, esophageal varices, other medical complications and death (Stimmel et al., 1972; Anglin et al., 1989). Higher death rates and medical illness have also been reported among alcohol-using patients on methadone (Rowan-Szal et al., 2000), with alcohol playing a significant role (Gossop et al., 2003). In hepatitis C infection, which is prevalent in patients on MMT, alcohol use causes more severe and rapidly progressive liver cirrhosis and hepatocellular carcinoma (Schiff, 1997).

It has been suggested that many MMT patients replace heroin with an increase of drinking (Anglin et al., 1989). Moreover, MMT patients who were also excessive alcohol users may need higher methadone doses (Ottomanelli, 1999), and also additional heroin and alcohol use can be reduced by higher methadone doses (Hartel et al., 1995; Maxwell and Shinderman, 1999). Some reports described the practice of "boosting," that is, combining the use of alcohol and methadone in order to obtain a qualitatively different euphoria experience that could not be obtained from either drug alone (Hunt et al. 1986). The interaction between alcohol and methadone metabolism has been evaluated and documented in several studies (see Kreek, 1990).

It has been suggested that MMT drinkers tend to engage in problematic community behaviors. Hunt et al. (1986) study results show that patients who were methadone-abusive drinkers were more likely to sell their methadone (16%) than the other methadone patients (10%). This behavior may elicit other interpretations, such as selling methadone to obtain money for drug purchases or additional alcohol consumption to alleviate the discomfort that resulted from selling a daily methadone dose (Ottomanelli, 1999).

In a study it was found that the methadone and buprenorphine treatment was able to suppress alcohol use in heroin addicts (Nava et al., 2008). This effect was more evident at the 6th and 12th month of treatment in the patients that received the highest doses of buprenorphine (32 mg/day). The mechanism underlying the effects of the OMT on the reduction of alcohol intake is still unclear although there are some promising theories. In the light of the above evidence, we hypothesize that use of the highest doses of buprenorphine could represent a potential effective treatment for heroin addicts with alcohol dependence and a possible therapeutic option in methadone-maintenance patients with an uncontrolled increase in alcohol intake. Another hypothesis is, the awareness of the potential influence of MMT on alcohol consumption is important, as early recognition and treatment of alcohol dependence in patients could have a major impact on treatment outcomes.

A previous research documented the considerable lack of treatment for alcohol related problems that occur among patients in methadone maintenance (El-Bassel et al., 1993). These patients may be further more vulnerable and should be identified and helped to achieve permanent abstinence (Dobler-Mikola et al., 2005). If MMT units do not have a clear policy for screening alcohol problems, it is truly possible that some heavy drinking patients may remain undetected in the treatment setting. Hence, clinicians should screen all methadone-using patients for alcohol abuse and dependence, and offer appropriate combined pharmacological and psychosocial treatment. For instance, Srivastava et al., (2008) study results noticeably suggested that methadone maintenance programs should prioritize addressing the issue of alcohol use and abuse in methadone maintenance programs.

However, despite the beneficial effects of methadone, it has been suggested in other studies that methadone treatment may lead to an increase in alcohol use and dependence (Green and Jaffe, 1977; Gelb et al., 1978; Kreek, 1984; D'Aunno and Vaughn, 1992; Backmund et al., 2003) which causes significant disability and places a large burden on health care resources. Thus, establishing the nature of the relationship between alcohol and opioids is important from a clinical perspective, as improved awareness would be useful in planning treatment for opioid dependent patients with concurrent alcohol use.

Schut et al.'s (1973) study of methadone outpatients asked participants about relative changes in alcohol consumption at different phases of drug use and treatment (first use of drugs, first use of narcotics, daily narcotic use, and on MMT treatment. Sixty-eight percent of patients reported that they did not use alcohol at all during daily narcotic use; however, after an average of 18 months on methadone treatment, only 38% reported not using any alcohol at all and 20% reported drinking more or much more than prior to treatment. Anglin et al. (1989), in their retrospective study of male heroin-addicted patients, found that alcohol consumption increased during methadone treatment. However, the authors concluded that the increased alcohol consumption observed in patients on MMT was not causally related to MMT because the increase was also observed in a non-MMT treatment group. They found an inverse relationship between alcohol use and narcotic use, i.e., alcohol use increased during any phase when opiate use decreased. The study included only patients who were no longer in treatment, suggesting that there would have been a time lapse between treatment and the time of the interview.

Fairbank et al. (1993) followed 513 heroin users admitted to MMT and found that there was a decline in the use of all substances (cocaine, amphetamines, tranquilizers, marijuana, and illegal methadone) at 1 year. Alcohol was a notable exception: Heavy alcohol use (defined as 5 drinks/day for the last 90 days) remained constant from pre-admission (28%) to follow-up 1 year later (26%), regardless of whether patients were still on methadone. Strain et al. (1996) randomized intravenous opioid-dependent patients to either buprenorphine or MMT and followed them for 16 weeks. The patients who were enrolled in the methadone arm did not have a statistically significant change at either 6 or 16 weeks in the alcohol component (including the number of days drinking to intoxication in the last 30 days) of their ASI (Addiction Severity Index) scores. Schottenfeld et al. (1998) also randomized patients to either methadone or buprenorphine and found that, after 22 weeks of maintenance, there was no significant effect of MMT on the number of reported days using alcohol and the number of standard drinks consumed. Gossop et al. (2000) followed a cohort of patients for a mean of 414 days and, using the UK Royal College of Psychiatrists' recommendations for sensible drinking, found that there was no change from intake to follow-up in the overall percentage of patients who were drinking above safe guidelines, although there was reduction in the use of illicit stimulant, benzodiazepine, or opiate. Strang et al. (2000) found that in their randomized controlled trial of patients randomized to oral or injectable methadone for 6 months, there was no change in the frequency of alcohol used in the last 30 days in either group, although benzodiazepine and crack/cocaine use decreased.

Chapter 3

3. NEUROPSYCHOLOGY OF DRUG AND POLYDRUG USE: A VIEW FROM RESEARCH STUDIES

ABSTRACT

Neuroscience studies frequently show that alcohol and drug abusers report cognitive impairments. However, the concomitant use of several psychoactive substances may perhaps disclose important confounds. In this chapter we present some of the most important neuropsychological and neuroimagiological findings in what concerns the consumption of a particular drug of abuse, namely, opiates, alcohol, cannabis and psychostimulants as cocaine. The simultaneous use of substances could produce conflicting results when we identify "a drug a choice". Some mixed results when considering polydrug use will be presented and methodological concerns in neuropsychological research studies will be exposed.

Keywords: neuropsychology; drug consumption; polydrug; cognition.

The advances in neuropsychological and neuroimagiological techniques have allowed a remarkable progress in the scientific knowledge of the addicted brain, particularly at the level of substance abuse processes. Research on drug consumption neurosciences achieved nowadays a robust agreement that drug dependence is undoubtedly correlated with deficiencies in cognitive functions.

When we consider polydrug use and abuse, deficits can be attributed to variability or/and cumulative dosage effects of drugs.

Neuropsychological research of chronic opiate abuse has been relatively limited with some mixed and controversial results (Yucel et al., 2007). Some studies report persistence neurocognitive deficits in recovering opiate addicts, while others found that abstinent addicts have no significant neurocognitive deficits. For instance, a study performed by Guerra et al. (1987), founded that current heroin abusers showed deficits in attention, working memory, episodic memory and verbal fluency, which normalized 7 to 14 days following rapid detoxification.

Chronic opiate users have been shown to have disturbances in neurocognitive regions when comparing to controls, in particular, in prefrontal cortical areas (Ersche et al., 2005). A study performed by Pau et al. (2002) examined the relation between heroin use and three frontal executive functions, namely, impulse control, attention and mental flexibility. The authors concluded that heroin use only has an adverse effect in impulsive control and did not have in attention or mental flexibility. Whereas others studies reported deficits across several domains as attention, working memory, planning, paired associate learning and visual pattern (Guerra et al., 1987; Ornstein et al., 2000; Ersche et al., 2005). For instance, Darke et al. (2000) study found that methadone-maintained heroin addicts performed more poorly on all neurocognitive tasks assessed, comprising domains like information processing speed, attentional capacity, visual memory, verbal learning, and problem solving. Neuroanatomical studies in chronic heroin users reported a significantly decreased grey-matter in the prefrontal cortex, superior temporal cortex, insula and fusiform gyrus (Lyoo et al., 2006). All these findings are in line with prefrontal dysfunction, elucidating why heroin users report so many difficulties when in front of reward-based decisions like drug consumption.

When considering cannabis abuse, neuropsychological studies demonstrated impaired performances on a variety of attention, memory, and executive function tasks (Solowij et al., 2002; Pope et al., 2003). Adding together, the neuroimaging studies corroborate these findings, showing modifications in prefrontal, basal ganglia, cerebellar and hippocampus regions (Eldreth et al., 2004). The extense of recovery of cognitive function following total abstinence of consumption has been an important and uncertainty issue in cannabis use literature. Some studies suggest no recovery after abstinence, while others report full or partial recovery after a phase of total abstinence.

Several studies have reported that psychostimulants (pe. cocaine, amphetamine and methamphetamine) abuse is associated with deficits in several cognitive domains. For instance, executive functioning, memory and visuoperception (Bolla et al., 1999; Yucel et al., 2007). For example, MDMA is recognized to disturb working memory and short-term memory (Verkes et al. 2001).

Studies demonstrate that chronic long term cocaine use is associated with dysfunctions in prefrontal cortex, namely lateral orbitofrontal; anterior cingulate, and cerebellum and with a reduced functioning of dopamine D2 receptors (Volkow et al. 1999; (Hester and Garavan 2004; Bolla et al. 2004). Other studies reported that cocaine induced a brain volumetric reduction in the prefrontal cortex even after 6 weeks abstinence (Fein et al. 2002) and that the continued cocaine use may arrest the normal white matter maturation (Bartzokis et al. 2000).

The deleterious impact of ethanol in the brain can promote powerful anatomical and physiological changes in the brain tissue, which can be mediated by direct neurotoxicity or indirect paths such as metabolic (accumulation of acetaldehyde), nutritional (deficit) or hepatic injury (Mann et al., 2001). Normally, these brain alterations induced by pathological alcohol consumption interfere with the natural history of alcoholism, disturbing the clinical evolution of the patients throughout the therapeutical process.

The study of the relation between the cognitive function and alcoholism has been generated frequently contradictory conclusions, probably due to the extensive heterogeneity of the samples evaluated, type of neurocognitive batteries applied, neuroradiologic methods, and the periods of abstinence after the beginning of alcohol detoxification.

Case-control neuropsychologic studies with alcohol dependent individuals have demonstrated with some consistency the presence cognitive impairments in memory, executive function and visuospatial tasks (Sullivan et al., 2000; 2002; Ambrose et al., 2001; Demir et al., 2002; Zinn et al., 2004). The disposal of these cognitive deficits seems to relate with multiple elements of the natural history of alcoholism, for example, the number of previous alcohol detoxifications (Duka et al., 2003); compulsive pattern of alcohol ingestion (Kokavec and Crowe, 1999); familiar history of alcoholism (Pessione et al., 1995); nutritional deficit (Lotfi and Meyer, 1989); personal history of alcohol consumption (Molina et al., 1994; Sullivan et al., 2002; Oscar-Berman et al., 2004) in last the 3 months (Horner et al., 1999); time frame of abstinence (Oscar-Berman et al., 2004). Beyond the plurality associated with the personal relation with alcohol, the neurocognitive functioning of alcoholics also seems to be subordinate to the phenotypic multiplicity of alcoholism disease.

Although it evidences the reversibility of cognitive deficits with total alcohol abstinence, the cognitive damage induced by alcohol can persist beyond the ceasing of alcohol consumption. It estimates that 45% of alcohol dependent subjects present residual neuropsychological deficits when evaluated 3 weeks after alcohol abstinence and 15% preserve these deficits throughout 1 year of abstinence (Rourke and Loberg, 1996).

Neuroanatomic studies in alcohol dependent populations have disclosed that the chronic exposure to ethanol leads to a series of neuroadaptative changes that modulate the pathophysiology of chronic alcoholism, namely, a diffuse cortical and subcortical atrophy with consequent increase of cerebral spaces filled by cerebrospinal liquid and reduction of the cerebral weight (Ratti et al., 1999; Harper and Matsumoto, 2005). The pattern of neurologic deficits induced by chronic alcoholism has been focused mainly in fontal lobes changes (Ratti et al, 1999), with findings of frontal hipoperfusion (Melgaard et al., 1993) left superior associated with early onset of alcoholism and of uniform hipoperfusion of the frontal lobe when considered the late onset of alcoholism (Demir et al., 2002). The deterioration of frontal lobe regions in alcohol dependent subjects seems to be associated with a worse clinic prognosis with a consequent increase of relapse rates during treatment (Roehrich and Goldman, 1993). For instance, O´Leary (1979) in a preliminary observation verified that patients with better cognitive performances tend to finish with success the inpatient treatments and showed less relapses rates and higher periods of abstinence.

Neuropsychological data also has been consolidated the association between alcoholism, mnesic disturbances and changes in limbic structures. To our days, it is consensual that the acute exposure to alcohol dramatically disturbs the neurophysiology of the hippocampus region and the functions that it is evicted, as memory and learning (Silvers et al., 2003).

During years of clinical practice, psychologists and neuropsychologists have examined the functional correlates of drugs potential toxic effect in brain in the figure of neurocognitive task performances. The fact that several psychoactive substance users are usually polydrug users led some researchers to abandon the traditional no-drug control group, using instead other methodologies to assess the link between drugs and cognitive function.

Until today, neuropsychological results in what concerns polydrug use patterns show us some interesting findings, revealing a few important confounds. Using a broad battery of sensitive neurocognitive tests, the study of Fishbein et al., (2007) showed that in most cases, heroin addicts are similar to alcoholics and alcohol + heroin dependent, in their presentation of several marked deficits relative to controls, which possibly will suggest that common mechanisms may be at play. Nevertheless, the study also showed that heroin addicts exhibited significantly more disadvantageous decision making and longer deliberation times while making risky decisions than the other groups. In another study, Stevens et al., (2007) evaluate chronic male polydrug abusers with opiate dependence and hypothesized some cognitive dimensions could be related to anhedonia, specifically, implicit learning and executive function. The study found in polydrug abusers a moderate impairment in implicit learning, acquisition, reversal and extinction of conditioned responses, of latent inhibition as well as anhedonia, while working memory was spared. In the abstinent group, cognitive performance was normal except for latent inhibition and more anhedonia and depression than in controls. Anhedonia was correlated with implicit learning but not with executive function. The authors conclude that these results may suggest that current polydrug abusers suffer from impairment of many cognitive functions and from anhedonia. Although, during abstinence, there is near normal cognitive function but still anhedonia. Rodríguez (1993) investigated the family history of alcoholism as a potential contributor to cognitive dysfunction in polydrug abusers. Results showed that polydrug users with positive histories tended to perform worse on several cognitive measures than those with negative family histories, but these tendencies were not statistically significant.

The chronic dual use of substances could produce conflicting results when we identify in subjects a pattern of use or "a drug a choice". For instance, Dafters et al., (2004) investigate whether long-term MDMA use or long-term cannabis use is responsible for the changes sometimes observed in recreational MDMA users. The results showed that subjects who used cannabis, with or without MDMA, showed deficits on three memory tests but not on any of the attention or taskshifting tests. These findings allow the authors to suggest that some previous reports of MDMA-induced memory problems may have been due to the effects of cannabis use that were not controlled for. Interestingly, concomitant cannabis use does not appear to intensify methamphetamine neurotoxicity, and has been suggested to have neuroprotective effects (Gonzalez et al., 2004). Recently, Colzato et al. (2009) tested whether the recreational polydrug use of cocaine is associated with a detectable selective impairment in cognitive flexibility and/or working memory. The study findings suggest that recreational use of cocaine selectively impairs cognitive flexibility but not the maintenance of information in working memory.

Multiple drug use generates complex neuropharmacological effects on the brain. In this line of research, Grant and Judd (1976) evaluated 66 polydrug users with EEG and a neuropsychological battery and founded that 43% had EEG abnormalities and 45% had neuropsychological impairment 3 weeks after admission. The authors suggest that cerebral dysfunction in polydrug users might be the result of organicity of intermediate duration and that deficits may be experienced by some beyond 5 months of reduced use or abstinence

In methodological terms, usually, neuropsychological studies carry out statistical correlations between the cognitive performance of subjects in neuropsychological tasks and the exposure to the "preferred drug of choice" and the other drugs, cautiously pointing the findings mainly to the consumption of the "drug of choice" and only secondarily to the use of the other drugs.

The presence of a multiple drug consumption pattern in drug abuse individuals clearly reduce the sensitivity in terms of utilized neuropsychological test batteries and the neuroanatomical loci specificity associated with cognitive functions.

Certainly, different drug consumption endorses different pharmacological effect in the brain and neurotoxicity and, as a consequence, displays a different representation of possible related cognitive deficits. For instance, although opiates were the preferred drug of use in one population, heroin polydrug users may also consume alcohol and cannabis (for example, in a weekly basis) and use also amphetamines, cocaine, barbiturates, steroids, or solvents. For this reasons, neuropsychological studies that include polydrug abusers carry serious limitations, taking into account that it is difficult to accurately distinguish between neurocognitive correlates of one drug versus the influence of other. For instance, the extensive use of alcohol could be particularly common and be found in most of the histories of substance abusers and many heroin addicts may be in contact with other opiate substances as methadone or buprenorphine. Therefore, neuropsychological assessments are somewhat restrict in their findings and posterior interpretations, in part due to the fact that many of these subjects get in touch with a plethora of psychotropic substances. All this may cause serious variations in the pattern of neuropsychological deficits of this multiple drug abuse phenotype and turn out to be almost impossible to isolate the potential cognitive deficits associated with one specific drug, even if it's the "drug of choice". After a careful revision of studies, Fishbein et al., (2007) concluded that (i) the association between chronic drug use and varying patterns of cognitive deficits may be a function of the differential effects of specific drugs largely on prefrontal brain circuits or prefrontal deficits that predated and possibly predisposed to drug abuse, (ii) current use of opiates and MMT, in particular, may be responsible for many of the deficits often found in addicts, and (iii) abstinence may promote some cognitive improvements in certain drug groups but not others, with mixed results for heroin users.

Chapter 4

4. MEMORY BLACKOUTS, ALCOHOL AND POLYDRUG USE: WHAT HAPPEN WHEN EVERYTHING IS BLACK?

ABSTRACT

Alcohol and drug use every so often causes memory blackouts. This amnesic episode induced by alcohol/drug consumption, during which the individual is conscientious, guided and able to participate in any type of activity, has been the main focus of many research studies among substance abuse populations. In this chapter we enunciate the most considerably etiologic risk factors; social and behavioral consequences associated and describe some of the most important laboratory findings. Data referring to the interface between polydrug use pattern and the mnesic vulnerability will be also discussed, above all, the synergic effect of substances in the brain.

Keywords: memory; blackouts; alcohol; risk factors.

Memory blackout occurrence is a common phenomenon in substance use population, mainly in alcohol abusers. Indeed, acute and chronic exposure to psychoactive substances like alcohol could disturb noticeably frontal lobe and hippocampus neurophysiology and related cognitive functions (Silvers et al., 2003).

For instance, an Alcoholic Blackout (AB) could be defined as an amnesic episode induced by alcohol consumption, during which the individual is conscientious, guided and able to participate in any type of activity.

Behavioral aspects associated to AB have demonstrated that during this period individuals engage in many complex activities, which may need physical and cognitive appropriate functioning. This fact demonstrates that, although during an AB episode the individual does not keep the succeeded in memory, the information kept in short-term memory level remains active, at least for some seconds. However, this information is not transferred to long-term memory. Only in this way it is possible to explain that during an AB, the individual can maintain appropriate conversations, drive motorized vehicles or participate in risk behaviors, which he cannot recall after. For instance, White et al. (2004) assessed young drinkers involved in activities during AB periods and verified that 78% reported being unable to recall how they got home; 42% became involved in some type of sexual relationship with knowing people; 32% woke up confused because they were unsure of where s/he were, or participated in an argument or fight; 12% became involved in sexual activities with unknown people; 10% damaged or vandalized property; 8% used drugs that normally would not use; 6% drove motorized vehicles and 2% were arrested. Details regarding the impact of an AB experience on student's emotional life found that, 50% revealed scared, 26% indifferent, 8% embarrassed and 4% worried or guilty. In what it concerns to alcohol consumption's impact, 58% reported that AB experience affected their alcohol consumption pattern, 93.1% started to drink more carefully and only 7% stopped to drink.

Oorsouw et al. (2004) concluded that the situations that were frequently extinguished from memory during an AB were: speak with other people, going somewhere, falling, feel embarrassed or to have embarrassed someone, drive vehicles, or become involved in some type of antisocial behaviors (fights, vandalism, heteroagressivity).

Numbers from memory blackout prevalence's demonstrate that is a common phenomenon in substance users, specially, alcohol consumers. In the general population, it was observed that the history of alcoholic blackouts during life was reported by 39.3% of women and 52.4% of men (Nelson et al., 2004). In adolescent populations, the values range from 51% (White et al., 2002) to 88% (White et al., 2004). In what concerns alcoholic populations, prevalence's fluctuate from 58% (61) to 94% (Tarter & Schneider, 1976).

The first scientific exposition about alcoholic blackout relates to Jellineck (1946). Through data collected from AA, the author verified that alcohol dependent individuals frequently reported alcohol induced blackouts, concluding that the occurrence of an induced amnesic period could classify a major indicator of alcoholism. Posterior studies had come to contest this conclusion, showing that memory blackout is an ubiquous phenomenon throughout all the alcohol consumers' populations, from young to adults and from moderate to dependent consumers (O'Mahony, 2004; Oorsouw et al., 2004; Tarter & Schneider, 1976; White et al., 2004). Although, it is important to declare that memory blackouts are not tied with the "healthful" use of alcoholic beverages, since it damages the natural development of human mnesic traits.

Historically, the empirical knowledge on blackouts advanced with studies handle for Goodwin et al. (1969) and Ryback (1970). The authors verified that the acute exposition to alcohol produce a syndrome manifestly analogous to the mnesic commitment generated by the injury of hippocampus, that is, a deficit in memory formation keeping the reevocation process of information unbroken. With this observation, the authors state that alcohol consumption could perturb the capacity to form new memories through the disturbance of the anatomo-cellular activity of hippocampus.

Several studies have showed that some individuals are more vulnerable to report memory complains related to substance induced blackouts than others. For example, Hartzler and Fromme (2003) verified that young adults who reported alcoholic blackouts showed a higher memory vulnerability to acute alcohol effect. While sober, the two groups had equal performance regarding memory tasks. Though, when moderately intoxicated (BAC = 0.08%), the group with alcoholic blackout history performed poorly in memory tasks, when compared with the population with no history of alcoholic blackouts.

Although the excessive consumption of alcohol mix frequently with the occurrence of memory blackouts, this fact by itself, does not delimit a cause-effect relation, nor explains the numerous occasions where an individual drinks in excess without loss of memory, or the reason for which some individuals with equitable alcohol consumptions show losses of memory and others not. Some questions come out. May some individuals be more prone to experience memory blackouts than other? Which will be the factors that increase or diminish the probability of blackouts occurrence?

Some laboratorial findings may help to answer these questions. For instance, Ryback in 1970 verified that 5 of the 7 hospitalized alcoholics did not recover some of the most significant events during the period of alcohol consumption in the previous night. In this study, the author observed that the individuals that had not reported episodes of alcoholic blackout experienced a paused and gradual ascent of the blood alcohol concentration (BAC); whereas those who reported memory blackouts showed a rapid increase of BAC. Supported by these results, Ryback (1970) concluded that the volubility of the BAC would be a key predictor for the occurrence of alcoholic blackouts.

The concomitant use of several psychoactive substances is also considered a major risk marker for memory disturbances. The polydrug use pattern provides the interaction of multiple psychoactive substances in the brain, that can by it self, or in society produce an amnesic effect. Data referring to polydrug use reported that the alcohol consumption associated to other drugs; amplify the vulnerability to experiment a blackout episode, especially, in block (Hartzler & Fromme, 2003). In literature, two qualitative types of blackouts are discriminated, in block and fragmented (Goodwin et al., 1969). Normally, in block blackouts requires higher blood alcohol concentrations and occurs with loss of memory for all events. The individuals that experience this type of blackout are incapable to remember any detail from alcohol intoxication period, being any effort of memory reproduction unfruitful. Taken into account the memory general model, we could say that happen an absolute blockade of the process of information transference from short-term information to long-term. A fragmented blackout is much more common than in block (Goodwin et al., 1969; Hartzler & Fromme, 2003; White et al., 2004), and involves the partial impediment of mnesic formation during the period of alcohol intoxication.

Moreover, the synergic effects of alcohol consumption associated with concomitant benzodiazepine use or with cannabis (THC) use, increases dramatically the probability of a mnesic effect occurrence (White et al., 1997; Ciccocioppo et al., 2002).

Some other conditions have been enunciated as risk factors for memory blackouts occurrence. Among them are: to drink with empty stomach; "binge drinking" (compulsory consumption of 5 or more drinks); consumption of " shot" drinks; to drink when tired; frequency of intoxications; past history of blackouts and the fast rise of BAC (Goodwin et al., 1969; Ryback, 1970; Poikolainen, 1982).

Genetic-epidemiologic research (Nelson et al., 2004), states that exists a residual genetic contribution for memory blackouts occurrence risk, even after controlling alcohol intoxication frequency during excessive alcohol consumption periods. The hereditary risk during life for alcoholic blackouts was 52.5%; and 57.8% for the occurrence of 3 or more blackouts in one year. Presumably, this specific genetic contribution for neurobiological vulnerability to alcoholic blackout, could derive from genes whose products are involved in the alcohol effect in hippocampus neurotransmission; in the transmission mediated by GABA-A receptors or/and, in the polymorphisms that are involved with NMDA receptors structure and sub-unities (Nelson et al., 2004).

To evoke a case of amnesia induced by drug consumption (pe., alcoholic blackout) could represent an sufficiently attractive strategy to minimize the legal responsibility of some criminal behaviors. Statistical numbers show that normally transgressors claim for some form of amnesia after perpetrated crimes (pe., sexual offenses), being the great part of the amnesic states imputed to extreme consumption of alcohol (Taylor & Kopelman, 1984).

During blackout, brain regions related to the organization of long-term memories are transitory "turned off", however, during this blackout stage; individuals could be enrolled in strategically complex activities such as interpersonal dialogues or drive vehicles.

Chapter 5

5. DEFINING ALCOHOL USE: SOMETIMES AS A BEVERAGE OTHER AS A DRUG

ABSTRACT

Alcohol use determines different brain effects. Occasionally origin euphoria whereas others causes relaxed or depressed states. Because alcoholic beverages are so widely consumed and accepted, in some cases is difficult to acknowledge that alcohol use could represent a drug. In addition, nowadays, an overabundance of alcohol use terminologies is used to illustrate the heterogeneous continuum between moderate alcohol use and pathological chronic use. This chapter was prepared with the intent to clarify this enormous density of conditions, which are included in a spectrum of pathological alcohol use. Indeed, several classifications of alcohol use will come into view, namely, the definitions of low-risk drinking, hazardous drinking and alcohol abuse and dependence.

Keywords: alcohol use, alcohol abuse, alcohol dependence.

Alcohol is by definition a depressant of the CNS, that is, slows down the activity of the brain. Habitual ethanol use determine a biphasic effect, with individuals normally experiencing a stimulant-like effects during the ascending limb of the blood alcohol concentration curve and lesser sedative-like effects on the descending limb of the blood alcohol concentration curve. In little doses, alcohol could make individuals to feel relax and decrease inhibitions, though, in higher doses, alcohol can origin unconsciousness or even be lethal.

The World Health Organization estimates that alcohol dependence is the third leading cause of disease burden in developing countries worldwide (WHO, 2004). Across the Europe, alcohol is responsible for between 6.8% (western) and 12.1% (eastern) of all years of health lost through premature death or disability (data based on disability-adjusted life years (DALYs) *(Room et al., 2005)*.

Drinking is one of the most common behaviors in modern societies. For the reason that alcohol is so widely used and cultural accepted, some individuals do not realize that in some cases alcohol use could represent a drug.

Alcohol dependence has been described a primary, chronic disease with biological, psychosocial, and cultural factors influencing its development and expression. *This disease* is the result of complex etiologic interactions, being particularly difficult to disconnect the relative contribution of each of these determinants in order to elucidate whether biological, psychosocial and cultural factors are the most dominant. It is well-known that alcoholism runs in families and is partly inherited. The findings suggest that the genetic familial transmission of alcoholism risk vary from 40 - 60% (Goodwin et al., 1973; Prescott & Kendler, 1999).

A plethora of alcohol use terminologies and manifestations are used at the present time to illustrate the continuum between moderate alcohol use and pathological chronic use. In order to elucidate this density of conditions, several classifications of alcohol use come into view.

The measurement of alcohol drinking practices has been found that alcohol use is a tricky variable to evaluate, define and classify. Indeed, a "universal" definition is rather important given that practitioners and researcher need to communicate in a common and understandable technical language.

In the spectrum of pathological alcohol use, the National Institute of Alcohol Abuse and Alcoholism (NIAAA) described Unhealthy Alcohol Use. Unhealthy alcohol use defines a range of disorders varying from at-risk drinking to alcohol dependence. The NIAAA recommends a single-question screen for unhealthy alcohol use. The recommended question asks, "How many times in the past year have you had X or more drinks in a day?" (where X is 5 for men and 4 for women). Another terminology is harmful and hazardous drinking. The consumption of alcohol at a hazardous level (at-risk drinking) means that the individual is drinking over the recommended limits (NIAAA consumption guidelines for low-risk drinking) and is for that reason more vulnerable to some kind of problem. Certainly, if an individual experiences an alcohol-related problem such as driving while intoxicated (DWI), or illness or social/legal problem, it has to be classified as a harmful/problem drinker.

Some papers mention the potential benefits associated with moderate drinking. For example, moderate drinking may perhaps be associated with reduced risk of heart attack or atherosclerosis. However, to discuss effectively these issues, we must clearly raise the questions, what is the meaning of such subjective term as moderate drinking? And what counts as a drink?

Alcohol content can fluctuate significantly, even though, these differences are smaller than we might expect. Taken into account that different types of alcoholic drinks contain different amounts of pure alcohol, we need to define a standard drink as one that contains 10-14g (it dependents on the country) grams of pure alcohol. For instance, a regular beer, a glass of wine or a glass of malt liquor could present different sizes; nevertheless, each contains approximately the same amount of alcohol and counts as a single (standard) drink.

Moderate drinking (or low-risk drinking, safe drinking) express how much individuals can drink without being at high risk of incurring negative consequences.

The NIAAA consumption guidelines for low-risk drinking are as follow: for Men; 2 standard drinks per drinking occasion or 14 standard drinks per week; and for Women (and people age 65 and over); 1 standard drink per drinking occasion or 7 drinks per week.

In the closing stage of the alcohol use continuum we discover the alcohol abuse and alcohol dependence disorders.

The figure 1 describes the spectrum of alcohol use disorders.

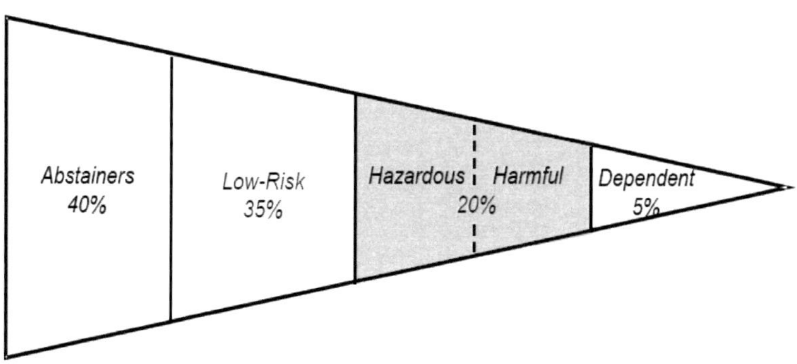

Figure 1. Spectrum of alcohol use.

Types of drinkers:

Abstainers: Drink no alcohol.
Low-risk Drink: Alcohol use does not involve health or other related problems.
Hazardous (At-risk): Alcohol use puts the individual at risk for injury/illness or social problems.
Harmful/Abuse: Currently experiencing problems related to alcohol;
Dependent: meet criteria for dependence

The International Classification of Diseases (ICD) from the World Health Organization (WHO) and the Diagnostic and Statistical Manual of Mental Disorders, Fourth Edition (DSM–IV-TR) published by the American Psychiatric Association are used worldwide for the classification of mental disorders. Both classifications provide diagnostic criteria for alcohol use disorders - dependence and abuse/harmful use.

DSM-IV-TR differentiated into three mutually exclusive categories: no substance use disorder, abuse only, or dependence.

Table 1 presents the criteria for substance abuse according to DSM-IV-TR

Criteria for Substance Abuse

A maladaptive pattern of substance use leading to clinically significant impairment or distress, as manifested by one (or more) of the following, occurring within a 12 -month period:

1. Recurrent substance use resulting in a failure to fulfill major role obligations at work, school, or home (such as repeated absences or poor work performance related to substance use; substance-related absences, suspensions, or expulsions from school; or neglect of children or household).

2. Recurrent substance use in situations in which it is physically hazardous (such as driving an automobile or operating a machine when impaired by substance use)

3. Recurrent substance-related legal problems (such as arrests for substance related disorderly conduct)

4. Continued substance use despite having persistent or recurrent social or interpersonal problems caused or exacerbated by the effects of the substance (for example, arguments with spouse about consequences of intoxication and physical fights).

Table 2 presents the criteria for substance dependence according to DSM-IV-TR

Criteria for Substance Dependence

A maladaptive pattern of substance use, leading to clinically significant impairment or distress, as manifested by three (or more) of the following, occurring at any time in the same 12 -month period:

1. Tolerance, as defined by either of the following: A need for markedly increased amounts of the substance to achieve intoxication or desired effect or Markedly diminished effect with continued use of the same amount of the substance

2. Withdrawal, as manifested by either of the following: The characteristic withdrawal syndrome for the substance or The same (or a closely related) substance is taken to relieve or avoid withdrawal symptoms

3. The substance is often taken in larger amounts or over a longer period than was intended

4. There is a persistent desire or unsuccessful efforts to cut down or control substance use

5. A great deal of time is spent on activities necessary to obtain the substance (e.g., visiting multiple doctors or driving long distances), use the substance (e.g., chain -smoking), or recover from its effects

6. Important social, occupational, or recreational activities are given up or reduced because of substance use

7. The substance use is continued despite knowledge of having a persistent physical or psychological problem that is likely to have been caused or exacerbated by the substance

The International Classification of Diseases (ICD-10) defines two alcohol use disorders - dependence and abuse/harmful use.

According to the ICD-10 the alcohol dependence syndrome is a "cluster of behavioral, cognitive, and physiological phenomena that develop after repeated substance use and that typically include a strong desire to take the drug, difficulties in controlling its use, persisting in its use despite harmful consequences, a higher priority given to drug use than to other activities and obligations, increased tolerance, and sometimes a physical withdrawal state" (World Health Organization, 1994).

Table 3 presents the criteria for Alcohol Abuse/Harmful Use Diagnostic according to ICD-10

Alcohol Abuse/Harmful Use Diagnostic Criteria according to ICD-10

(A) [Harmful use] Clear evidence that alcohol use contributed to physical or psychological harm, which may lead to disability/adverse consequences

(B) The nature of harm should be clearly identifiable (and specified)

(C) The pattern of use has persisted for at least 1 month or has occurred repeatedly within a 12–month period

(D) Symptoms do not meet criteria for any other mental or behavioral disorder related to alcohol in the same time period (except for acute intoxication

Table 4 presents the criteria for Alcohol dependence Diagnostic according to ICD-10

Alcohol Dependence Diagnostic Criteria according to ICD-10

(A) Three or more of the following: occurring together for at least 1 month, or if less than 1 month, occurring together repeatedly within a 12–month period:

(B) Duration Criterion: Three or more of dependence criteria occurring for at least 1 month, or if less than 1 month, occurring together repeatedly within a 12–month period.

Tolerance: Need for significantly increased amounts of alcohol to achieve intoxication or desired effect; or markedly diminished effect with continued use of the same amount of alcohol

Withdrawal: Physiological symptoms characteristic of the withdrawal syndrome for alcohol; or use of alcohol (or closely related substance) to relieve or avoid withdrawal symptoms

Impaired Control: Difficulties in controlling drinking in terms of onset, termination, or levels of use; drinking in larger amounts or over a longer period than intended; or a persistent desire or unsuccessful efforts to reduce or control drinking

Neglect of Activities: Important alternative pleasures or interests given up or reduced because of drinking

Time Spent in Alcohol - Related Activity: A great deal of time spent in activities necessary to obtain, to use, or to recover from the effects of drinking
Continued Use Despite Problems: Persisting with drinking despite clear evidence and knowledge of harmful physical or psychological consequences

Compulsion: A strong desire or sense of compulsion to drink

In 1976, Edwards and Gross projected a novel syndrome with a remarkable clinical validity: the Alcohol Dependence Syndrome (ADS). According to the authors, dependence becomes a feedback behavior comprising several components. Hence, the elements of ADS are: 1) Narrowing of the drinking repertoire; 2) Importance of the behavior of searching alcohol; 3) Increase in alcohol tolerance; 4) Repeated symptoms of abstinence whereas there is a decrease or interruption of alcohol consumption; 5) Relief or avoidance of abstinence symptoms by increasing alcohol ingestion; 6) Subjective perception of the need of drinking and 7) Reinstallation after abstinence. This concept suggests that the severity of dependence lies on a continuum, with more dependent individuals manifesting a superior number and a greater intensity of symptoms.

Chapter 6

6. Substance Abuse Phenotypes: An Update of the Substance Abuse Multivariate Typologies

Abstract

Efforts have been made to discriminate substance abusers in more homogeneous subgroups in order to amplify research knowledge and promote treatments efficacy. Multivariate statistical models introduced several of the most important classification schemes in the alcoholism and drug addiction literature. In this chapter we describe the binary models of Cloninger and Babor, the Lesch Alcoholic Typology based in chronic predictors of alcoholism and the five type model of the NETER Alcoholic Typology. We will see in detail the classification procedure of the NAT scheme. Further, we focus in the commonalities among different subtyping classification systems and provide particular consideration to polydrug subtypes. This type of research aspires to clarify one the most essential attributes in the alcoholism research field, the heterogeneity of alcoholic behaviors.

Keywords: alcoholism; typologies; subtypes; classification procedures.

Substance abuse literature has pointed to the need for taxonomies for classifying different types of addictive behaviors. Over the past decades, many efforts have been made to differentiate substance abusers in more homogeneous subgroups, in order to better predict the future course of the disorder, the accuracy of psychological and neurobiological mechanisms and to promote treatments response effectiveness (Babor & Caetano, 2006; Dvorak et al., 2006; Pombo & Lesch, 2009). These methodologies used multivariate statistical models that take into account the synergetic effects of neurobiological conditions, personality traits, co-morbidity prevalence's, alcohol consumption patterns, psychopathology and other drug consumptions. The vast majority of this type of research focused in alcoholic individuals, with the purpose to elucidate the heterogeneity of alcoholic behaviors and resolve a probable treatment matching strategy. We pointed some of the most important typology models released in the alcoholism literature, using treatment-seeking alcohol dependent patients.

Binary Models

Historically, Jellinek (1960) was the first to apply a modern scientific approach of the alcohol problem, systematizing 5 alcoholics types, from which, type 3 (Gamma) and type 4 (Delta) are pointed out in clinical terms. Gamma alcoholics presented acquired tissue tolerance, physical dependence (withdrawal), and loss of control. Delta alcoholics are characterized by gamma features and also an incapability to abstain from drinking.

Using data from a cross-fostering study of Swedish adoptees, Cloninger et al. (1981) identified two divergent forms of alcoholism based on differences in alcohol related symptoms, patterns of family transmission and personality characteristics – the so-called type I versus type II dichotomy model. Type I drinkers, also called *milieu-limited,* are characterized by a slow progression to pathological drinking, more often beginning after 20 years of age. Type II drinkers, also called *male-limited,* distinguished a precocious onset of alcohol consumption with a swift progression to dependence, associated with a marked impulsiveness and antisocial behavior. Cloninger´s et al. (1981) clearly achieved two patterns of family influences in alcoholism "transmission", with type II patients showing more genetic vulnerability to develop an alcohol problem, when comparing to type I alcoholic patients. Until our days, Cloninger´s et al. (1981) study remains one of most important studies in alcoholism hereditability field.

This dicothomic approach has been validated by biologic and psychosocial measures. For example, Pombo et al., (2008a), in a Portuguese alcoholic outpatient sample, verified that Cloninger's type II patients showed lower levels of alcoholism psychological denial, when compared with type I. Reports also reveal different levels of a potential trait biomarker for alcoholism as Platelet MAO-B activity, with type II alcoholism showing low levels of platelet MAO-B activity when comparing with to type I (von Knorring et al., 1985, 1998; Pandey et al., 1988; Sullivan et al., 1990). Recently, MAO-B was related to hostility and cognitive nonverbal reasoning in type I alcohol dependent patients (Pombo et al., 2008b).

Efforts to discriminate Cloninger´s *et al.* (1981) type I/type II approach have introduced several classification schemes. The table 5 provides an overview of the clinical criteria for subtyping the Cloninger approach according to von Knorring *et al.* (1985); Sullivan *et al.* (1990) and Gilligan *et al.* (1988).

Table 5 - clinical criteria for subtyping the Cloninger approach according to von Knorring et al. (1985); Sullivan et al. (1990) and Gilligan et al. (1988)

von Knorring et al. (1985) criteria:

Type I
presence of subjective drinking problems start after age 25
first treatment contact after age 30
few social complications (legal, work problems)

Type II
subjective drinking problems start before age 25
first treatment contact before age 30
frequent social complications (legal, work problems)

Gilligan et al. (1988) criteria:

Type I
guilt about drinking
binges or benders
tried to set limits
liver disease
onset of drinking problems after age 25

Type II
fights when drinking
driving under influence of alcohol or has alcohol-related motor vehicle accidents
problems abstaining
treatment other than Alcoholics Anonymous
Sullivan et al. (1990)
Type I

presence of subjective drinking problems start after age 25
first treatment contact after age 30
few social complications (legal, work problems)
negative history of family alcoholism

Type II
subjective drinking problems start before age 25
first treatment contact before age 30
frequent social complications (legal, work problems)
positive history of family alcoholism

At the beginning of the ninety decade, Babor et al. (1992) proposed a typology derived from 17 dimensions that summarize the information from his sample of alcohol-dependent subjects. Based on a clusters analysis, the authors extracted a binary solution (Type A and Type B) that diverge in several key dimensions as familial alcoholism, childhood disorder, dependence syndrome and antisocial personality disorder. Indeed, Babor *et al.* (1992) considered that type A subjects were characterized by low alcoholism family risk, low social alcohol related problems, mild alcohol dependence level and mild associated psychopathology. Type B subjects were recognized by the presence of high alcoholism family risk, high alcohol dependence level, consumption of other drugs and psychiatric comorbidity.

In our days, literature accepts two basic phenotypes of alcohol dependent drinkers, defined as low-severity/vulnerability subgroup and high-severity/vulnerability subgroup. As Babor & Caetano (2006) state, low-severity/vulnerability subgroup is characterized by later onset of problem drinking; few childhood risk factors; relative absence of alcohol problems in family history; low level of antecedents of psychopathology and less severe alcohol consumption, alcohol dependence and alcohol related problems. In opposite, the high-severity/vulnerability subgroup is characterized by an early onset of problem drinking; greater childhood risk factors; family history of alcoholism problems; antecedents of psychopathology and severe alcohol consumption, alcohol dependence and alcohol related problems. In this binary classification, low-severity/vulnerability alcoholics are in some way similar to Cloninger et al. (1981) type I and Babor et al. (1992) type A, and high-severity/vulnerability alcoholics are similar to Cloninger et al. (1981) type II and Babor et al. (1992) type B.

From a historical viewpoint, Babor et al. (1992) and Carpenter and Hasin (2001) hypothesized two mythological categories of problem drinkers: the Apollonian-Dionysian distinction. According to Carpenter and Hasin (2001),

Apollonian drinkers (less severe alcoholic type) develop an alcohol problem inside a context of socially approved heavy drinking with a more benign cluster of alcohol problems. This subgroup is also defined by a later onset of alcoholism; slower development course; fewer complications and better prognosis. Dionysian type (more severe alcoholic type) is defined by pathological drinking in a context of more severe biopsychological problems; early onset of alcoholism; psychological vulnerability; more severe complications; greater familial and genetic influences and worse prognosis.

LESCH ALCOHOLIC TYPOLOGY (LAT)

The Lesch Alcoholic Typology (LAT) emerged from a long-term follow-up study of 18 years, with prospective follow-up investigations after 12 months, after 5 years, after 18 years. This model describes predictors for chronic alcoholism development, distinguished four evolutionary types depending on family history of alcoholism, previous personal psychopathology and neurobiological substratum. The descriptors for each type are as follow: Type I (called model of allergy): social drinking develops to habitual drinking, medium abstinence syndrome occurs early, craving, positive family history for alcoholism and minimal social effects; Type II (called Anxiety Model, Alcohol as conflict-solver): alcohol consumption as a coping strategy against anxiety, suicidal intentions (mainly under the influence of alcohol) and no severe somatic alcohol related disorders or withdrawal; Type III (called Depression Model, alcohol as Anti-Depressant): alcohol consumption as a form of self treatment (depression, sleep disorders), suicidal tendencies, psychiatric co-morbidity, aggressive behavior even without alcohol and mild somatic withdrawal; and Type IV(called Habit Forming Model, Pre-Alcoholic Cerebral Damages and Infantile development Disorders): cerebral disturbances or prenatal damage before the termination of brain development, grand mal seizures (not only during withdrawal), enuresis nocturnal, deterioration of individual's psychic, organic and social sphere. Thus, type I evidences the appearance of early withdrawal symptoms and craving, which can be associated with an endorphinical vulnerability. Type II shows suicidal intentions, anxiety and premorbid conflicts, with changes within the serotoninergic system. Type III typifies an aggressive and impulsive behavior with the existence of psychiatric comorbidity. In this type a chronobiological change can be previewed. And finally, type IV shows premorbid organic cerebral lesions associated with a deterioration of individual's psychic, organic, and social sphere (Lesch et al. 1988; Dvorak et al., 2006; Pombo & Lesch, 2009). The predictors which had been found were integrated into a decision tree that is nowadays available as a computer program in most European languages and it could thus be used within various international multicentre therapy studies. . The table 6 provides an overview of the diagnostic process of the Lesch Typology.

Lesch et al., (1988) 4 subtype distinction were validated by neurobiologic, psychological and psychophysiologic measures and psychopharmacologic trials (Dvorak et al. 2006; Lesch et al. 2001; Walter et al. 2006; Pombo et al. 2007; Hillemacher & Bleich, 2008).

Table 6. Decision tree for the Lesch Typology

Basis for the diagnostic process of chronic alcoholism for the typology of Lesch's types 1 – 4.

This alcoholism subtype classification was conventioned in an exclusion way, beginning with type IV, followed by type III, I and II.

Lesch Alcoholic Typology classification logarithm:

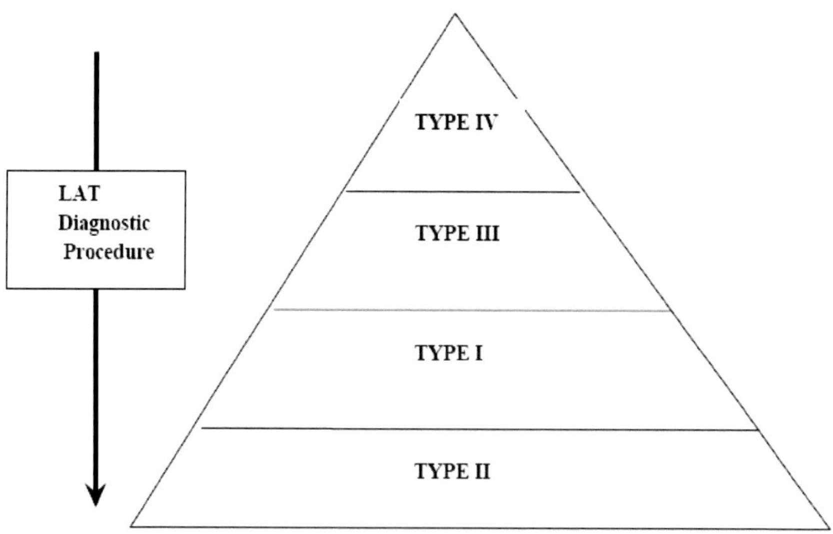

NETER Alcoholic Typology

Recently, was published the NETER Alcoholic Typology (NAT), a model that was achieved based on alcohol dependent outpatients recruited from the alcoholism unit (NETER) of Santa Maria's Universitary Hospital in Lisbon, Portugal (Cardoso et al. 2006). The authors concluded a factorial structure organized in 5 dimensions: anxiopathic type, typifies anxious functioning; heredopathic type, congregates familial and environment influences on alcoholism; thimopathic type, related to affective symptomatology; sociopathic type, characterized by social disruptive behaviors under; and adictopathic type, connected to younger individuals who consume alcohol and other types of psychoactive substances.

Cardoso et al. (2006) describe the 5 subtypes of alcoholics as follows: Anxiopathic type is a group whose alcoholic behaviors are modeled by anxious personality traits, providing a variation in the alcohol consumption pattern, behavior and emotionality. Withdrawal from alcohol can lead to aggressive behavior, sometimes in relation to directed alcohol-seeking behavior. Heredopathic type congregates alcoholism family influences with a low education and economic level. The Thimopathic individuals correspond to a group with psychopathology problems in affective life. In these cases, alcohol consumption is used as a form of self-treatment for the negative affects. The authors also found a close relationship between the depressive dimension and alexithymia component in this group. The Sociopathic subtype determines a group with a longest number of years drinking, showing the coexistence of one of the most prevalent comorbid conditions among alcoholics: the antisocial behavior. The Adictopathic is a polydrug alcoholic subtype.

As the typology authors concluded (Cardoso et al. 2006), this 5 type solution may derived from the interactive complexity between genetic/family and psychosocial factors of the societies in evolution, which might result in more alcoholic polymorphic subtypes.

To validate a typology it becomes indispensable that the subtypes differentiate (discriminant validity) in some terms of external criteria (variables not enclosed in the typology item selection) and positively correlates with measures of the same construct (convergent validity). Convergent and discriminant validity of NAT was confirming by the agreement with Lesch et al. (1988) subtypes and by the distribution of external measures of gender; tobacco; alcohol syndromes, alcohol related problems severity; psychological and behavior dimensions (Pombo et al., 2007).

For the NAT decision process, the classification process between the 5 alcoholic subtypes was developed taking into account the scores of each variable which corresponds to a specific alcoholism subtype (internal criteria). This alcoholism subtype delimitation was conventioned in an exclusion way, beginning with Adictopathic followed by Sociopathic, Thimopathic, Anxiophatic and Heredopathic. Each subtype presents exclusiveness conditions: 1st – Adictopathic (N5; "polydrug type") – if the patient presents a lifetime history of heroin or cocaine dependence, the adictopathic type should be diagnosed. 2nd – Sociopathic (N4; "antisocial type") – if the patient presents a severe history of antisocial behavior and legal problems, the sociopathic type should be diagnosed. 3rd – Thimopathic (N3; "affective type") - : if the patient presents a lifetime history of major depression episodes, the thimopathic type should be diagnosed. 4th – Anxiopathic (N1; "anxious type") – if the patient presents a lifetime history of anxiety disorders, the Anxiopathic type should be diagnosed. Anxiety symptoms have to be differentiated from symptoms related to alcohol withdrawal. 5th – Heredopathic (N2; "inherited type") – if the patient presents a high prevalence of family history of alcoholism (first or/and second degree), the heredopathic type should be diagnosed. If any of the previous exclusion conditions have been selected, use a quantitative procedure with the conditions that are aggregated to each subtype. The table 7 provides an overview of the diagnostic process of the NETER Alcoholic Typology.

Table 7. Classification procedure of the NAT scheme

See in detail the classification procedure of the NAT scheme.

NETER Alcoholic Typology classification logarithm:

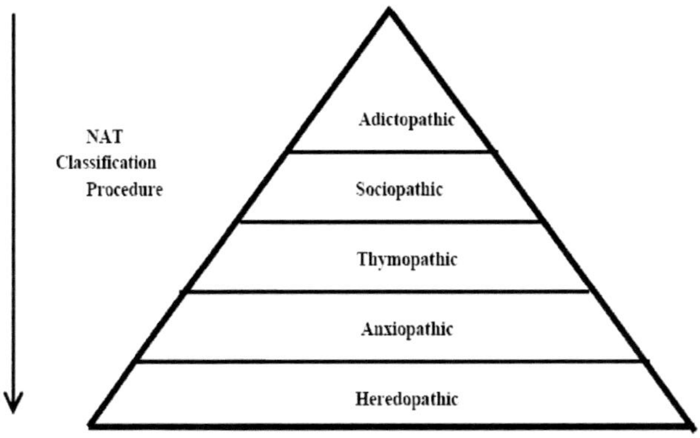

The scoring methods are as follows: for a highly marked condition add 3 points (+3), if the condition is only present add 1 point (+1), and if it's not present remove 1 point (-1). The total score obtained in each alcoholism subtype will be translated to a final categorical type. Scores equal to 0 are indicators of classification absence. (For more details see Cardoso et al. 2006 and Pombo et al. 2007).

Adictopathic "polydrug type"
1. Other types of psychoactive drugs consumption - Lifetime illicit drug consumption namely, heroin, cocaine, cannabis ☐ 2. Disruptive behavior during childhood and/or adolescence - Previous social and relational problems, such as relationship difficulties in school and with authority figures, and being involved in fights with colleagues. ☐ 3. Younger individuals (≈ 20 and 35 years) ☐ TOTAL ☐
Exclusion criteria: if in the condition 1 (Other types of psychoactive drugs consumption) the person presents a lifetime history of heroin or cocaine dependence, the adictopathic type has to be diagnosed.

Sociopathic "antisocial type"	
1. Early contact with alcohol beverages (≈ 5 and 14 years)	☐
2. Aggressive behavior during alcohol consuming - Socially disturbed behavior such as verbal aggressiveness, irritability, and physical violence to things or others.	☐
3. Legal problems Participation in illegal activities such as drunk driving, having been arrested due to public intoxication, adult criminality, or aggressive acts.	☐
TOTAL ☐	
Exclusion criteria: if in the condition 2 and/or 3 (Aggressive behavior during alcohol consuming; Legal problems) the person presents a severe history of antisocial behavior, the sociopathic type has to be diagnosed.	

Thimopathic "affective type"	
1. Alexithymia - Describes an inability to talk about feelings due to a lack of emotional awareness	☐
2. Depression - Depressive mood, decrease of energy, feelings of helplessness and guilt, loss of interest or pleasure in activities	☐
3. Work problems - Absenteeism, reduced productivity, alcohol-related accidents in workplace, reduced work performance, unemployment, and loss of working time	☐
TOTAL ☐	
Exclusion criteria: if in the condition 2 (Depression) the person presents a lifetime history of major depression episodes, the thimopathic type has to be diagnosed.	

Anxiopathic "anxious type"	
1. Neuroticism - Persons with a tendency towards neuroticism are more worried, temperamental and prone to sadness.	☐
2. Anxiety – Symptoms such as palpitations, anger, irritability, lack of concentration, nervousness, tension, mood swings.	☐
3. Craving -Powerful urge to drink or intense thoughts about alcohol	☐
4. Aggressive behavior when sober – Verbal aggressiveness (shouting), dysphoric mood (angry, impatient), physical violence to things (destroying things)	☐

TOTAL ☐
Exclusion criteria: if in the condition 2(Anxiety) the person presents a lifetime history of anxiety disorders, the Anxiopathic type has to be diagnosed. *Comment: anxiety symptoms have to be differentiated from symptoms related to alcohol withdrawal.*

Heredopathic "inherited type"	
1. Positive Family History of Alcoholism - Alcoholism family influences from parents, grandparents	☐
2. Severe dependence of alcohol – Symptoms such as rapid heart rates, sweating, decreased appetite, difficulty in sleeping, generalized seizure, high fevers, delirium tremens	☐

3. Low social class - Social classes with a low education and economic level	☐
TOTAL ☐	
Exclusion criteria: if in the condition 1(Positive Family History of Alcoholism) the person presents a high prevalence of family history of alcoholism (first and second degree), the heredopathic type has to be diagnosed.* ** if any of the previous conditions have been selected*	

Alcoholism Classification according to NETER ALCOHOLIC TYPOLOGY (NAT)

Commonalities among Different Subtyping Classification Systems

Empirical research showed that there is a significant overlap across many of the multivariate alcoholic subtypes purposed. For instance, as we mention before, Cloninger et al. (1981) type I and Babor et al. (1992) type A; and Cloninger et al. (1981) type II and Babor et al. (1992) type B, are in some way similar.

In a recent paper, Pombo & Lesch (2009) published a detailed cross-sectional analysis obtained from a sample of 318 alcohol dependent patients recruited from the alcoholism unit (NETER) of the Psychiatric Service of Santa Maria University Hospital in Lisbon (Portugal). The study was conducted in order to investigate alcoholic patient's classification concordance among six multidimensional alcoholic typological models: Cloninger´s Type I/II von Knorring, Sullivan and Gilligan operationalized criteria; Babor Type A/B; NAT and LAT subtypes. Results showed a significant overlap across many of the multivariate alcoholic subtypes purposed, in which much of the concordance is a function of common characteristics in subtype operationalization. According to the authors, these results agree with Hesselbrock and Hesselbrock (2006) conclusions, when they put emphasis on the fact that in spite of diverse theoretical backgrounds of the researchers, the samples examined and the methods used to structure the typology, there is a remarkable similarity across many of the multivariate alcoholic typologies purposed. Hesselbrock and Hesselbrock (2006) suggested four main phenotypes of alcoholism: chronic/severe type, depressed/anxious type, mildly affected type and an antisocial type.

For Pombo & Lesch (2009), there are several aspects of typologies definitions and validity that need to be considered. For instance, different distinction strategies for subgrouping alcoholics could display heterogeneous data and may jeopardize results from clinical and psychopharmacological trials that use subgrouping procedures in research methods.

Attention to Polydrug Subtypes

As Cardoso et al. (2006) pointed; alcoholics with concomitant polydrug use reflect a hybrid subgroup not devoted most of the time to a particular psychoactive substance. The authors called this particular type of patients as

Adictopathics. Indeed, the lifetime diagnosis of joint alcohol and drug abuse is high, with most common alcohol/drug combinations related to alcohol with cocaine, alcohol with marijuana, and alcohol with sedatives (Martin et al. 1996; Staines et al., 2001). Normally, this alcoholic polydrug life-style, which may involve the active involvement in drug networks, drug dealing, sex trading, promiscuity and other behavioral problems; may engage the patients in health risks associated with Sexually Transmitted Diseases (STD) and HIV infections (Windle and Scheidt, 2004; Cardoso et al., 2006). For instance, viral chronic hepatitis could represent a major problem in these patients. It is well identified that alcohol abuse plays a role as a co-morbid factor in the development of liver damage and disease progression. Gitto et al., (2009) concluded that alcohol abuse has a strong negative influence on the fate of patients with viral chronic hepatitis, as it is associated with an accelerated progression of liver injury, leading to an earlier development of cirrhosis, and higher mortality. It also could impair the response to interferon treatment.

Considering the potential usefulness of alcoholism subtyping systems and the current generalization of polydrug consumption pattern among substance use populations, it will be an indispensable concern how these constructs perform in other substance abuse disorders. For example, recently, Pombo & Lesch (2009) found that addictopatic patients from NETER classification scheme, an alcoholic polydrug subtype, significantly positive correlate with Cloninger´s subtype II.

With the intent to assess the replicability and generalizability of multidimensional alcoholism typological systems in other substance use disorders, Ball et al., (1995) support the Babor´s distinction of type A and type B in sample of cocaine abusers. According to the results of the study, 33% of the cocaine abusers were classified as type B, presenting higher rates of pre-morbid risk factors, more severe drug problem, concomitant alcohol abuse and psychiatric comorbidity; when comparing with 67% of participants categorized as type A.

Chapter 7

7. Psychological Assessment for Addictive Behaviors: A Review

Abstract

Several psychometric instruments to evaluate alcohol and drug addiction behaviors are currently available. Some are used as screening tools to identify preliminary signs of hazardous drinking or drug consumption and others are used to assist clinicians to explore and create a much more comprehensible picture of patient's alcohol/drug-related difficulties. In this chapter we focus on the most applied and internationally tested instruments in alcoholism field, with particular attention to the following assessment fields: screening of problem drinking, alcohol use and alcohol related problems, Relapse Risk Situations and Cognitive Resources and Motivational Resources.

Keywords: psychometric instruments, assessment, alcohol, screening.

A - Alcoholism:
1. Assessment Field:
Screening of Problem Drinking

Alcohol related morbidity and mortality are common in health institutions, mostly general hospitals or primary care settings. However, much admitted alcohol related disorders remain undetected, in to some extent due to time constraints. As a result, to aid the identification of such patients, we call for brief instruments that could in an uncomplicated and trouble-free manner discover patients at risk for developing alcohol related problems.

Screening instruments were designed to serve as a quantifiable measure of alcohol problems. The application of this type of instruments provides to the clinician a useful tool for the early diagnosis of alcohol abuse/dependence and can allow early therapeutic interventions. Nevertheless, screening tests only should be used to screen alcohol use problems and it cannot be used alone to diagnose an alcohol disease. These instruments only suggest that an alcohol problem could be present, being required other type of instruments to diagnose alcohol dependence (e.g., clinical interview).

In sum, screening instruments are tools that manifestly focus on the identification of preliminary signs of hazardous drinking and mild dependence. Some of the most used instruments in alcoholism literature that has been tested internationally in primary care settings with high levels of validity and reliability are the Michigan Alcoholism Screening Test (MAST), the CAGE questionnaire and the Alcohol Use Disorders Identification Test (AUDIT).

Most of these instruments are already available in alcohol and drug addiction governmental websites.

1.1. Michigan Alcoholism Screening Test (MAST)

Developed by Selzer (1971), the MAST is one of the most widely used instrument for the assessment of alcohol related problems, been used as a screening epidemiological tool in quite a lot of prevalence surveys.

This scale composed by 25 weighted yes/no items (binary choice questionnaire), takes normally 10 to 15 minutes to be completed. Ranging from 0 to 53, the total score contributes toward an overall indication of alcohol abuse severity.

Trough MAST, we can evaluate and discriminate how much the alcohol use can affect patient's life, particularly in psychic, physical and social domains (family, Work, behavior).

According to Selzer (1971) cut-point scores, a total score of 0 through 3 indicates social drinking, 4 was suggestive of an alcohol problem (borderline), and a total score of 5 or more clearly correspond to an alcohol problem. A more practical scoring system is generally used in clinical settings; in what a score equal or greater to 7 signify a possible alcohol problem.

1.2. CAGE

CAGE questionnaire was designed by Ewing in 1984. To apply this instrument you only need to ask the individuals these 4 questions:

1 - Have you ever felt you should cut down on your drinking?
2 - Have people annoyed you by criticizing your drinking?
3 - Have you ever felt bad or guilty about your drinking?
4 - Have you ever had a drink first thing in the morning to steady your nerves or to get rid of a hangover?

Indeed, "CAGE" questionnaire is basically an acronym for Cut down, Annoyed, Guilty and Eye opener. The scoring system of this instrument is also very simple: Two "yes" responses suggest an alcohol problem.

This screening tool is very short and simple to administer. For instance, CAGE questions could incorporate in a usual clinical interview.

1.3. AUDIT (Alcohol Use Disorders Identification Test)

The Alcohol Use Disorders Identification Test (AUDIT) was developed by the World Health Organization (WHO) in order to screen patients with alcohol related problems.

Studies have been showed that the AUDIT is a very reliable and sensitive tool to the early detection of hazardous drinking.

This transcultural instrument is constituted by three questions on alcohol consumption (1 to 3), three questions on drinking behavior and dependence (4 to 6) and four questions in what concerns the consequences related to drinking (7 to 10). The items are scored from 0 to 4 with a maximum total score of 40. Normally, if the patient gets a total score equal or above 8 points s/he is at risk for alcohol problems.

2. Assessment Field: Alcohol Use and Alcohol Related Problems

A plethora of personal and inter-personal life domains can be affected by alcohol and drug consumption. Some patients report legal problems (e.g., drive under alcohol influence), family conflicts, conjugal discussions, cognitive complaints (e.g. memory disturbances), work problems (e.g., unemployment), physical diseases (e.g. cirrhosis) or mental health disturbs (e.g., depression, anxiety, suicide). Indeed, clinicians and researchers need an effective tool to discriminate a typology of alcohol related problems in order to delineate a much more comprehensible picture of patient's alcohol-related difficulties. In addition, this evaluation also supplies the assessment of the problem severity and assists therapist interventions. However, always keep in mind; the most effective tool for diagnosing alcohol related problems is with a detailed history of the personal drinking behaviors.

A further essential assessment point in drinking history relays to alcohol use estimates. When you consider this issue, one question come to the surface – how much is too much? For that reason, it's important to know whether your drinking quantification is safe or risky. The foremost technique of gathering this information is with retrospective drinking self-reports.

A number of questionnaires have been developed to measure alcohol use and alcohol related problems, including Drinker Inventory of Consequences (DrInC), the Quantity–Frequency (QF) Methods, and the Alcohol Timeline Followback (TLFB).

2.1. Drinker Inventory of Consequences (DrInC)

The 50-item Drinker Inventory of Consequences (DrInC) was developed to assess the overall level of drinking-related consequences in five areas. Each scale provides a lifetime and past 3-month measure of adverse consequences. In addition, scales can be combined to assess total adverse consequences. The DrInC is applied in a pencil and paper self-administered format. Psychometrics findings of the DrInC indicate that is a reliable, valid, and clinically useful instrument (Miller et al., 1995).

2.2. Quantity–Frequency (QF) Methods

Quantity-Frequency (QF) methods have been used for obtaining self-reports of drinking. As Sobell & Sobell (2003) mention, QF methods ask respondents to estimate the average number of drinking days over a certain period and then to estimate the average number of drinks consumed per drinking day. After that, the product of those measures is calculated.

2.3. Alcohol Timeline Followback (TLFB)

The Timeline Followback (TLFB) is a scientifically and clinically useful tool for assessing substance use (Agrawal et al., 2007). The TLFB is a Daily Estimation method, developed three decades ago as an assessment instrument for obtaining retrospective estimates of alcohol consumption using a calendar format. The TLFB can be administered by an interviewer using a paper and pencil format, self-administered, administered by computer, administered by telephone, and administered by therapists and researchers.

The TLFB can be used to evaluate the representativeness of different time windows for describing annual drinking data, which interfere with the average time to administer. For example, a 90-day TLFB typically takes about 5 to10 minutes to complete, while a 360-day TLFB will take about 20 to 30 minutes.

The instruments showed good psychometric characteristics, in what concerns for test-retest reliability (stability), concurrent validity and construct validity.

TLFB feedback information seems to have value as an intervention as well as an assessment instrument. Researchers and clinicians desiring to use the TLFB can download materials and instructions free of charge by going to *www.nova.edu/gsc* on the internet and clicking on "online forms."

3. Assessment Field: Relapse Risk Situations and Cognitive Resources

There is progressing and systematic concern among clinicians and researchers about the high rate of relapse in addiction patients.

Alcohol related expectancies have been implicated in the beginning and maintenance of alcohol consumption. Many studies about alcohol beliefs and expectations and alcohol consumption report commonly this simple conclusion: the greater the expectancy, the greater alcohol consumption.

Additional elements in psychotherapeutic relapse prevention programs include craving management and coping skills refusal training. Without a doubt, one of the most "incredible" experiences in addiction is craving. Craving generally refers to the desire or urge to experience the effect of a previously experienced psychoactive substance.

Exploring carefully dimensions like high-risk relapse situations and related cognitive resources could represent nowadays an elementary concern in addiction treatment in order to better predict and prevent relapses. For instance, in cognitive-behavioral intervention models, patients could be assisted to create a profile of past drinking activities and current expectations about high-risk situations.

Some of the psychometrically sound measures to assess relapse risk situations and cognitive resources include the Alcohol Effects Questionnaire (AEQ), the Situational Confidence Questionnaire (SCQ), the Yale-Brown Obsessive Compulsive Drinking Scale (Y-BOCDS), the Penn Alcohol Craving Scale (PACS), the Alcohol Expectancy Questionnaire (AEQ), the Drinking Refusal Self-Efficacy Questionnaire (DRSEQ) and the Inventory of Drug-Taking Situations (IDTS).

3.1. Alcohol Effects Questionnaire (AEQ)

AEQ is 42-item questionnaire developed by Southwick et al., (1981). AEQ measures person's beliefs about alcohol in a series of statements that illustrate possible effects of alcohol use, presuming that alcohol sometimes or always has a stated effect. In this questionnaire, the person is invited to read each of the statements and respond according to the experience with a heavy drink occasion. Here are some examples of possible statements: Drinking makes me feel flushed; Drinking makes me feel less shy; I'm more romantic when I drink; I can't act as quickly when I've been drinking; Alcohol can act as an anesthetic for me; that is, it can deaden the pain; Drinking increases my aggressiveness; After drinking, I'm a better lover; Alcohol helps me sleep better.

3.2. Situational Confidence Questionnaire (SCQ)

The SCQ is a state dependent measure that assesses self-confidence to resist the urge to drink heavily or use drugs in a variety of situations (Annis, 1987).

This instrument was created on the grounds of Marlatt and Gordon's approach of relapse determinants, which comprises eight situations: (1) negative emotional states; (2) negative physical states; (3) positive emotional states; (4) testing personal control; (5) urges and temptations; (6) interpersonal conflict; (7) social pressure; and (8) positive emotional states. The SCQ asks people to imagine themselves as they are "*right now*" in each of the eight situations distinguished above. Then, they are asked to indicate on a visual analog scale how confident they are at the present time that they can resist the urge to drink heavily or to use drugs in each of the situations. Individuals are solicited to place an "X" along the line, from 0% ("not at all confident") to 100% ("totally confident"). Here we present some of the situations or events of the SCQ in which some people experience a drinking problem: I would be able to resist the urge to drink heavily if I had trouble sleeping; felt confident and relaxed; convinced myself that I was a new person and could take a few drinks; everything were going well; wanted to celebrate with a friend; were angry at the way things had turned out; felt nauseous; suddenly had an urge to drink; unexpectedly found a bottle of my favorite booze.

Currently, it also exist a brief version of the Situational Confidence Questionnaire, constituted only by 8 items (Beslin et al., 2000).

3.3. Yale-Brown Obsessive Compulsive Drinking Scale (Y-BOCDS)

The Yale-Brown Obsessive-compulsive Drinking Scale for heavy drinkers (YBOCDS-hd) was developed by Modell et al. (1992) in order to measure obsessive and compulsive characteristics of alcohol consumption.

This instrument is constituted by two sub-scales (obsessive and compulsive) that contain 5 items each and a total score based in the sum of both sub-scales. Obsessive and compulsive dimensions include time spent on obsessions/compulsions, interference from obsessions/compulsions, distress from obsessions/compulsions, resistance to obsessions/compulsions and control over obsessions/compulsions. Higher scores in the scale indicate an upper obsessive and compulsive behavior toward alcohol consumption.

This self-report questionnaire version, modified from the Yale-Brown Obsessive Compulsive Scale, was found to be related to alcohol craving and was able to differentiate between social drinkers and alcoholics (Modell et al. 1992).

3.4. Penn Alcohol Craving Scale (PACS)

The Penn Alcohol Craving Scale was designed by Flannery et al. (1999) as a craving assessment tool. Is a brief self-administered instrument, with a multi-item uni-factorial structure that consists in 5 items. The three first questions say respect to the frequency, intensity and duration of thoughts toward alcohol consumption, the fourth question asks for the subject resistance capabilities when alcohol is available and the final question says respect to the average level of craving during the last week. The items are scored from 0 to 6.

This scale has showed good psychometric qualities in what concerns reliability (Cronbach = 0.92), concurrent, predictive and discriminant validity (Flannery et al., 1999).

3.5. Alcohol Expectancy Questionnaire (AEQ)

The Alcohol Expectancy Questionnaire (AEQ) was developed by Brown et al., (1980, 1987) to evaluate cognitions related to alcohol use. The AEQ is one of the most psychometrically sound measures to assess alcohol related expectancies in adults and also in adolescent populations. Allen and Wilson (2003) found good psychometric features in what concerns reliability (test–retest and internal consistency) and validity (predictive, concurrent).

AEQ measures positive alcohol expectancies and generates six factor scores. The factors incorporate: global positive changes; sexual enhancement; physical and social pleasure; increased social assertiveness; relaxation and tension reduction; and arousal and power. Respondents answer to each item taken into account the agreement or disagreement with the statement. The greater the scale score, the greater the expectancies.

3.6. Drinking Refusal Self-Efficacy Questionnaire (DRSEQ)

The Drinking Refusal Self-Efficacy Questionnaire (DRSEQ) was designed by Young et al. in 1991. This instrument measures the belief about the person's ability to resist alcohol. Is a 31-item tool of drinking-related self-efficacy, constituted by three factors that are: drinking in situations characterized by social pressure, opportunistic drinking, and emotional relief (Young et al., 1991). The scale items assessed the participants' temptation to drink in several situations. For example, under social pressure (e.g., in a bar), for emotional relief (e.g., depressive feelings) or when presented with the opportunity (e.g., observe a glass of wine). Higher scores designate a higher level of refusal self-efficacy.

3.7. Inventory of Drug-Taking Situations (IDTS)

Developed by Annis & Martin (1985), the Inventory of Drug-Taking Situations (IDTS), is a 50-item self-report questionnaire that provides a profile of the situations in which an individual has used a substance of abuse. The drug-taking situations assessed on the IDTS are based on Marlatt's 8-category classification system of common antecedents to drug use. The IDTS offer for each client a split profile of the situations in which a client has used a particular drug above the past year. The individual is assessed in relation to eight categories of high-risk situations: Unpleasant Emotions (UE), Physical Discomfort (PD), Pleasant Emotions (PE), Testing Personal Control (TC), Urges and Temptations to Use (UT), Conflict with Others (CO), Social Pressure to Use (SO), and Pleasant Times with Others (PT). IDTS also present a second order factor constitute by three global categories: 1. (N) Negative situations (combining UE, PD and CO); 2. (P) Positive situations (combining PE and PT) and 3. (T) Temptation situations (combining UT, SO and TC). Clients are asked to specify their frequency of drug use or heavy drinking in the past year. The IDTS is designed to assess the situational antecedents to the use of a wide variety of drugs (e.g. alcohol, cocaine, heroin, other narcotics, cannabis, hallucinogens, tranquilizers, sedative/hypnotics, solvents, stimulants), and could be used as both research and clinical tool (Turner et al., 1997).

4. Assessment Field: Motivational Resources

Cognitive processes related to client motivation are important mediators of alcoholism treatment outcome.

Nowadays, in addiction clinical practice, is mandatory the match between the therapeutical intervention with the patient' readiness to change. Evaluating the individual's motivation to change his/e drinking behavior may help to define a clinical intervention with a higher likelihood of being effective.

The transtheoretical model of behavior change_provides a good general framework for research on client motivation. The transtheoretical model assumes that intentional behavior change involves passing through a sequence of five discrete stages: (1) precontemplation, (2) contemplation, (3) preparation, (4) action, and (5) maintenance. The model posits that individuals addicted to drugs typically cycle through a sequence of discrete stages before achieving sustained abstinence or moderation.

A number of self-administered questionnaires have been developed to assess an individual's "readiness to change". Some of them are the Stages of Change Readiness and Treatment Eagerness Scale (SOCRATES), the UNIVERSITY OF RHODE ISLAND CHANGE ASSESSMENT SCALE (URICA) and the Readiness to Change Questionnaire (RCQ).

4.1. SOCRATES (Stages of Change Readiness and Treatment Eagerness Scale)

SOCRATES is a 19-item self-administered instrument that was developed by Miller and Tonigan in 1996.

Initially, SOCRATES was designed to measure four "stages of change": precontemplation, contemplation, determination, and action. Though, a later version of the SOCRATES included eight additional items designed to measure the maintenance stage of change. Many studies recommend the use of a shorter version of SOCRATES taken into account that this shorter version of the SOCRATES was shown to perform as well as the longer version, and have a clearer factor structure.

Here we present some of the items included in the scale: I am actively doing things now to cut down or stop drinking; I'm not just thinking about changing my drinking, I'm already doing something about it; I was drinking too much at one time, but I've managed to change my drinking; I really want to make changes in my drinking; My drinking is causing a lot of harm; There are times when I wonder if I drink too much.

4.2. University of Rhode Island Change Assessment (Urica) Scale

URICA is a 32-item self-administered questionnaire to measure motivation to change. This instrument comprises a 4 subscales structure that analyzes the stages of change: Precontemplation, Contemplation, Action, and Maintenance (DiClemente & Hughes, 1990).

Responses are given on a 5-point Likert scale ranging from 1 (strong disagreement) to 5 (strong agreement).

This scale allows clinicians to assess Readiness to Change at treatment entrance.

Each scale statement describes how a person might feel when starting therapy. Here are some of the examples: As far as I'm concerned, I don't have any problems that need changing. I think I might be ready for some self-improvement. I am doing something about the problems that had been bothering me. It might be worthwhile to work on my problem. I'm not the problem one. It doesn't make much sense for me to be here.

4.3. Readiness to Change Questionnaire (RCQ-TV)

The 12-item Readiness to Change Questionnaire (RCQ) developed by Rollnick *et al.* (1992) was designed to represent a specific stage of change according to the transtheoretical model of Prochaska and DiClemente (Prochaska and DiClemente, 1986).

The RTC has been shown to have a three-factor structure (Rollnick *et al.*, 1992), corresponding to the three stages of change: Precontemplation, Contemplation and Action. Respondents follow five answer alternatives: totally agree, partly agree, unsure, partly disagree and totally disagree.

After obtaining each factor score, subjects are allocated in one of the three stages based on the factor highest score. We could also calculate a scale total score (one-factor model) combining all 12 items which represent a readiness score.

B. Drug Addiction

It's generally acknowledge that addicted individuals who seek for treatment have impairments across multiple domains of life functioning and could present multiple substance abuses.

The Drug Abuse Screening Test (DAST) and the Addiction Severity Index (ASI) are two of the most widely used instruments to assess substance abuse that clinicians should be aware, providing a brief screening of drug use and a comprehensive assessment of substance associated problems.

1. Drug Abuse Screening Test (DAST)

The DAST was developed in 1982 by Skinner as a brief, easy, and practical screening tool for the identification of psychoactive substance abusing individuals. This 20-item self-administered questionnaire takes about five minutes to complete.

The DAST helps subjects to become more aware of their use or abuse of drugs providing a quantitative index score of the degree of problems related to drug use.

Through the studies, the DAST has exhibited valid psychometric properties as a valid and sensitive screening instrument for the abuse of drugs other than alcohol. Factor analysis showed that the DAST is essentially a uni-dimensional scale

Screening test score ranges: 0, None; 1 to 5, Low Level; 6 to 10, Moderate Level; 11 to 15, Substantial Level; 16 to 20, Severe Level.

2. Addiction Severity Index (ASI)

ASI is probably the most commonly used assessment instrument in substance abuse clinics.

The Addiction Severity Index (ASI) design by McLellan et al., (1980) is a standardized instrument used to identify and assess alcohol and substance related problems.

This multidimensional diagnostic instrument (ASI) comprises approximately 150 questions divided in functional life key areas that have been widely shown to be affected by the substance abuse: medical status, employment and support, drug use, alcohol use, legal status, family and social status, and psychiatric status.

The main purpose of this semistructured tool is to create a problem severity index.

After the work of more than 15 years, the ASI has been translated into a quite a lot of languages, namely, Japanese, French, Portuguese, Spanish, German, or Dutch.

To our days, a numerous scientifically robust studies has been generally supporting the psychometrically qualities of reliability and validity of the ASI as an effective instrument for identifying the severity of addiction. Currently, the ASI has reached its fifth version.

Chapter 8

8. Psychology and Psychotherapy in Drug Addiction. Work Models of Drug Abuse

Abstract

Psychological interventions in drug abuse are complex but at the same time highly challenge. Drug abusers are a very mixed population with a wide variety of treatment needs. Normally, offering nearly everything to everyone is not the best way to rehabilitate these patients. Indeed, programs need to become clinically-driven, which means that only offers the services that the client really needs, no more than as long as they are needed. In this chapter we reflect about psychological interventions in drug abuse, considering different models to define and contextualize the psychosocial recovery. The psychodynamic and cognitive-behavioral approaches will be the main focus of reflection. Psychological intervention for drug addiction is also a challenge to the mentality and resilience of the therapist, which has to be flexible, creative and have confidence in his work.

Keywords: psychodynamic, addiction, cognitive-behavioral, psychotherapy.

The Complexity of Psychological Interventions in Drug Addiction

Until now, treatments for several addictions have included different kinds of rehabilitation programs, specifically, therapy and counseling, recovery groups as Alcoholics Anonymous or Narcotics Anonymous, and pharmacotherapies like drug substitution maintenance programs. However, in many cases, these methods present relatively high rates of recidivism. Hence, there remains an imperative need for new, more successful and efficient treatment methods (Krupitsky et al., 2002).

Commonly, the process of therapy is divided into three continuous stages: “detoxification”, “rehabilitation”, and “return-to-society”. Detoxification focus in relieving or eliminating syndromes caused by body dependence, which has no actual effect on drug seeking behavior caused by psychic dependence. Rehabilitation accepts drug addicts as patients to treat, while also taking the necessary steps to control the withdrawal syndrome which leads to mental sufferings and often to relapse. The rehabilitation stage is not only the key to recovering physical and mental health but is an essential element for abstainer’s return to the society (Yan et al., 2008).

Studies indicate that the persistently negative psychological attitudes of drug abusers directly affect the effect of detoxification therapy, rehabilitation, and maintenance of abstinence (Ziang & Wang, 1992). Therefore, in order to enhance detoxification effect, we should intensify psychological intervention within the environment of drug abuse treatment center, which will allow great improvements in drug abusers mental health and a reduction in their incapacitating psychological symptoms.

Until our days, psychological treatments for substance abusers have been underutilized, principally when compared to pharmacological interventions as opiate therapeutic substitution (methadone maintenance treatment or buprenorphine). In a first view, we may reflect that pharmacological approaches may yield results more clear, viable and effective. Nevertheless, today it’s consensual that a combine treatment (pharmacological and psychological) plays a substantial key role in abstinence maintenance and relapse prevention.

When we reflect about psychological interventions in drug abuse, it is important to consider some aspects that may be important to define and contextualize in treatment: the psychosocial recovery. There is growing evidence that drug abuse grounds is on the brink of shifting from longstanding pathology to a solution focused on recovery paradigm. In medical terms, recovery is a term that connotes a return to health following trauma or illness. The boundary of recovery concept in the drug abuse area is greatly dependent of each one understanding of what is recovering from.

Recovery in drug addiction could be defined as the experience through which individuals, families, and communities impacted by drub addiction, utilize internal and external resources to voluntarily resolve these problems, heal the wounds inflicted by drug addiction-related problems, actively manage their continued vulnerability to such problems, and develop a healthy, productive, and meaningful life. Recovery, characterized as a process, experience and a sustained status, is in this genuine meaning a deeply personal route of change, filtered by dimensions of age, gender, ethnicity, sexual orientation, cultural affiliation, degree of religiosity, and particular life-shaping experiences (e.g., personal or historical trauma). The experience of recovery can be either a climactic, health-inducing event (positive, irrevocable, permanent) or marked by time-sustained improvements in health and functioning (Cunningham, 2000; Granfield & Cloud, 1999).

In terms of substance abuse, the definition of recovery is dependent on the drug addiction approach (i.e. behavioral, spiritual, pharmacological). By principle, recovery in drug abusers will focus on the relationship that the individual maintain with the substance of abuse and the dynamic of the substance in their lives. Thus, drug abusers are motivated and assisted to stop the consumption of drugs and find alternatives to deal with drug addiction, new coping mechanisms, and new strategies that are more appropriate. Moreover, recovery should be enlarging to one's entire relationship with psychoactive drugs, rather than in reference to a single substance.

Any definition of recovery should link the concept to a previous clinical state, taken into consideration that drug abuse exists on a continuum from drug abuse abstinence, no problematic drug abuse, subclinical drug abuse (transient problems not meeting severity or persistence criteria for a substance use disorder), and two broad ending diagnostic entities as substance abuse and substance dependence. An ideal definition of recovery would be broad enough to embrace both incremental and transformative styles of recovery initiation and consolidation.

Normally, patients engage in different styles of recovery: with and without treatment, with and without medication, with and without mutual aid involvement. Others get involved with religious or spiritual organizations. All these diverse patterns of recovery provided differences in relational styles and identity in recovery process (White and Kurtz, 2006).

In many cases, to be successful in recovery, the process should avoid restricting the boundaries of healing to a particular and unique problem, framework, strategy, or style. For instance, if we face drug addiction as one of many problems of a person, perhaps as more visible and identifiable problem, the prospect of recovery would invariably change. With this perspective we would have to identify which other problem disrupts the person, as well as drug addiction: an inability to manage emotions, difficulty in interpersonal relationships, dealing with psychiatric disorders (i.e., depression, anxiety), difficulties in family dynamics, existential doubts. Therefore, the focus of the intervention would not only be the drug addiction but also other aspects of emotional, psychological or psychiatric conditions that have to be recovered.

Recovery must focus on the individual as a whole, and should include the different areas that constitute a person: physical, psychological, relational, social, family, work and spiritual. This holistic understanding is ambitious but also realistic, since drug addiction could affect all the areas of a person's life.

The complexity and heterogeneity of the human being as well as drug addiction, it will be a challenge to elect a type of psychological intervention that responds adequately to all these extremely intricate issues.

A "one size fits all" approach has historically dominated the standard treatment of drug abusers who have generally been informed, regardless of who they are as individuals, that life-time abstinence, usually coupled with the social support of other former addicts, is the only viable treatment option. While these recommendations have helped many individuals, particularly those with severe addictions, they do not address the experience of all substance abusers (Waltman, 1995).

Drug abusers come from a very mixed population with concomitant forms of psychopathology intertwined with substance abuse and have a wide variety of treatment needs. A common error is to try and offer nearly everything to everyone over fixed periods of time, that is, they are program-driven. This drives the program's cost up and strains the client's ability to comply. Instead, programs need to become clinically-driven, which means that only offers the services that the client really needs, no more than as long as they are needed (Waltman, 1995).

Some authors (Waltman, 1995) consider the following key ingredients for effective treatment of addictive disorders. They consist of: easy accessibility, treatment flexibility, collateral involvement, good therapists, motivated clients, matching treatment to salient client variables, client accountability for their sobriety, focused treatment approaches, and the follow-up of drop-outs and program graduates.

Treatment effectiveness depends on many variables other than the treatment modality alone. These include: the client's characteristics, the severity of the substance-abuse disorder, the relative potency of the intervention, the duration of treatment, the content of sessions, the process/course of treatment (Waltman, 1995).

Both psychoanalytic and cognitive-behavioral practitioners have often viewed substance abuse as an isolated problem within the individual requiring a referral to a specialized drug addiction programme, even when the therapist and patient have firmly established psychotherapeutic relationship (Miller & Brown, 1997). This response may be influenced by the addictive and destructive quality of the abused substances which tend to cause various real-life problems and significant complications. These issues are often thought to obstruct the psychotherapy process and are often referred out or "relegated" to the domain of generalized care management or unspecified "supportive" psychotherapy.

Programs should offer a basic complement of substance abuse treatment services including: interactional group therapy, sobriety skills training (e.g., relapse prevention, relapse recovery, and affect management), addiction education, individual therapy, family/marital therapy, medication, and case management.

The need of a thorough, independent and comprehensive emerges, to allow a more effective and more appropriate treatment. Hence, different areas of people's lives should be contemplated: system of beliefs, attachment styles, emotional regulation (management of emotions, alexithymia) interpersonal relationships, stressful life events, and coping mechanisms, in order to realize what the best approach is for each person.

Besides focusing on substance use and related psychological problems, clinicians should assess for other social service and medical care needs and arrange for attention to these needs. Some research supports the greater effectiveness of treatment plans that address multiple areas of need, rather than solely the presenting substance use disorder (McLellan et al., 1997).

Extensive research suggests that the most effective treatment programs are clear and well organized, actively involve clients in the program, provide a supportive and emotionally expressive environment, and emphasize self-direction, work, and social skills development (Haaga et al., 2006).

A treatment for drug addiction has to take into account some characteristics, which are not universal, of these individuals, but due to circumstances brought about by drug addiction, are commonly present in a high percentage of individuals. Drug abusers have: a low tolerance for frustration, often demand an immediate response, a rapid and effective solution; thought is formatted for the short term rather than medium-and long-term; may comprise marked cognitive impairment; recovery will deprive them of an immediate source of pleasure. Thus, the treatment involves a change of perspective, to live life according to another rhythm, according to other rules, a change that is not immediate, it takes time. For many people this change is extremely frustrating, eventually boycott the recovery.

Viewing substance use disorders as chronic and relapsing conditions suggests the need for a long-term perspective on the process of change, and an accompanying long-term plan to foster maintenance. Although treatment may be time-limited, a long-term maintenance plan should be integral to any treatment (Haaga et al., 2006).

In sum, therapists should access the profile of problems that the client brings to treatment, in order to select the appropriate treatments for multiple problems, search for a good timing and sequencing of provision of multiple treatments, and manage the complexity of delivering more than one empirically supported treatment when elements of the treatments may be contradictory.

It is clear that drug abusers structure their lives in a way that drug and drug-related behaviors becomes their "central activity" (Fingarette, 1988) or "core role" (Kelly, 1955). The addict role becomes well elaborated and inclusive, tightly woven into the person's construing of self and others. Concurrently, the drug abuser individual's construction of the self in other roles and contexts diminishes. Drug addiction typically has a profound impact upon many areas of an individual's functioning and experience. Psychosocial treatment is given to drug abusers and is usually available from a specialist service offering interpersonal, motivational, or cognitive-behavioral therapies, or a combination, with no specific medication component. During three to 20 sessions tailored to the client's needs, (National Treatment Agency for Substance Misuse, 2006) therapy aims to resolve ambivalence about change, improve recognition and control of drug use cues and urges, reduce drug-related harm, and prevent relapse. Increased intensity treatment, sometimes with educational and life-skills training, is delivered as a 12-week programme with 3–5 days' attendance per week. Psychosocial treatment is given by trained practitioners on an individual or group basis, and the client's partner or family can also participate. Indeed, psychosocial treatment is the recommended community intervention for addiction disorder.

Most prominently, therapeutic techniques should be provided within the context of a well-developed working alliance in therapy that is structured and goal-directed. These characteristics appear to be universal among all effective psychotherapies for drug addiction.

Beyond the working alliance, empirical research suggests that a number of specific therapeutic essentials are distinctive of effective treatments in drug addiction. There is modest evidence for the differential effectiveness of individual versus group therapy for treating drug abusers. However, given the social–interpersonal nature of drug abusers and the importance of the social environment to the successful resolution of these disorders, involvement of a significant other, looks to be helpful in contributing to the effectiveness of treatment. Similarly important is explicitly helping the client restructure his or her social environment in ways that support change. Positive outcomes are made more likely by facilitating involvement with social networks supportive of abstinence, such as a specific supportive family member, sponsor, or peer; and by helping the client access social environments supportive of abstinence (Haaga et al. 2006).

Extending the Concept of Addiction to Psychodynamic Considerations

For decades, psychodynamic views of addiction have been advocating the uniqueness of each individual, and trying to avoid general extrapolations. There are plenty of psychoanalytic perspectives on drug addiction; focusing in assumptions as object relations, difficulty in autonomy, problems in identity and defense mechanisms. Others highlight on disturbances in affect tolerance and regulation, narcissistic problems, and undersupplied intrapsychic functions.

For instance, object relation theory proposed that occur among drug addicts a replacement of the relational object, which is inaccessible, in which substance is perceived as illusory and controllable, defined as an immediate need. As a relationship guided by love, all the value of self is transported to the object relationship, to which all sense of existence is channeled, without which you can not survive. The required subject is quickly changed the subject to demanding. The substitute is the lover that only demands, and that slaves the drug addict, in this sick relationship.

For the drug abuser, and in particular to the destructive part of his personality, the essence is the power of this "thing" (substance) that he needs to incorporate, because he evaluates it as something good. There is however a partial and bad idealized object, although supposedly transformed into ideal. The need for this internalization is strong, and urgent, as the drug abuser feels he has nothing good on him.

According Pagés-Berthier (2002) the substance will therefore play the role of internal containing object. This state of narcissistic dependence can thus be constituted from the earliest stages of psychic maturation, favoring after a fragility of object relations and the possibilities of identification. To Pagés-Berthier (2002), in this condition of "transitive object" the drug comes as partial object that provides the individual an illusory sense of being all-powerful. The addict will, in this way, deny the importance of human object and subject to the "economy" of ambivalence towards the beloved. This narcissistic, pathological defense mechanism, results in a wound in the Ideal of the self, self-esteem and sense of personal identity. The auto erotic retreat protects the person from the other, moving away from relationships with others and the unpredictable reactions of the object.

There is no reciprocity with the drug, the drug abuser no longer know what is going to have. The narcissistic wound of rejection or loss is not therefore to be feared. So the drug represents an escape forward of the precariousness of the relationship of object. Paradoxically, it is, in short, to establish a passionate relationship with a thing devoid of conscience, instead of risking suffering the rejection of a loved one. The drug will always be there, and it would not reject the drug abuser.

According Bergeret (1983), for the drug abuser it is a void of fantasy and imagination, in a place where it should be located a representation of an object, significant other; the person feels more or less unconsciously, that this place is empty and that this place should be the image of someone. In the absence of a possibility of representing an object, the drug abuser looks for partial and secondary object in the substance, expecting to place in such poor condition that is bound to be illusory.

Some psychodynamic author's focuses on the aspect of autonomy in the drug abuser, which faces serious difficulty in feeling alone, without too much trouble, given the demands of reality. The drug abuser can not treat himself, can not feel good and valued, to build his future with autonomy, facing realistically the tasks of living. The need for the drug addiction demonstrates the failure of the mental resources necessary to ensure their own well-being, which is why it is "dependent". The drug abuser is not able, by means of mental resources, to ensure a sense of psychological well-being, of inner unity, and capacity and competence to face the tasks of life. The need for the drug corresponds to the inability to support a state of intense suffering inside and could translate a comprehensible poverty of an inner world. Therefore, it's a failure on the autonomy of the management of emotions, is an emotional dependence, since the drug abuser is unable to deal with and contain the emotions and affections.

There is a divestment of the individual in the mental resources which he could use to find an alternative solution. Simply, this path is much harder and longer than the path you have to do to find the nearest dealer (amputate their capabilities, slashed the future).

Resort to drugs to solve the mental suffering is to create a dependency on an object with which you can not make identification.

The achievement of an emotional autonomy has the influence of parental roles, individual resources, life events, and social interactions. Some of these individuals start with drug addiction during the phase where they should be searching and constructing an independent self. This process is destroyed by the substance that takes over the life of the drug abuser. Now, he has to face two problems of autonomy: from the drug and emotional autonomy.

Another perspective in understanding drug addiction is the difficulty in the identity in these patients. With low self-esteem and a diminished sense of personal identity, drug abusers "cling" to the drug for drunkenness. In pursuit, sometimes desperate, for a lost identity. Olivenstein (1987) says that the drug abuser fears not the lack of heroin, but the lack / failure prior to the drug exposes, is suffering from addiction.

To Pagés-Berthier (2002), these people compulsively switching between fullness and emptiness seem to be a common condition of its psychic survival. The practices that they deliver lead them, paradoxically, to test the limits of his body and his ego to the point where they take the place of their identity.

The commitment to a deviant "career" is consistent with people looking for identity, searching for other methods of social inclusion, particularly within groups of drug abusers. Drug addiction can often provide a group identity, as a standard model, to the detriment of the singularity and unity of the individual Bergeret (1983) finds that adolescents who use drugs are looking for images of parental identification increasingly difficult to find. They desesperately need a model of identification. To Olivenstein (1982), when the drug abuser finds a drug, it serves as completeness to his fragmented identity. Although the drug brings the embarrassment, this has a positive function, reducing the enormous embarrassment in which he lived before his meeting with the product, which was the embarrassment of not-being.

The use of the substance, when the pleasure ceases to be ubiquitous, is to sort. Wherever there was only painful uncertainty, there is now a certainty of repetition. The demand for control of the source of pleasure, apart from the uncertainty, that is almost always annoying.

Several other psychodynamic statements consider the drug as an anti-depression, using substances that act as substitutes for oral gratification and basic needs. Indeed, drug consumption gives the "fantasy" of a good mental and psychic functioning, which may perhaps end in an illusion of having an inner world of good quality induced by the eradication of insufferable feelings. Rado (1933) pointed that, from the "anxious depression", the painful tension is relieved by the "product" that, because of their pharmacological nature, relieves suffering, promotes the welfare and inflates narcissism.

Inflated with his size (omnipotence), the ego is unable to acknowledge its own destruction, becoming also decreased in the consciousness of self and other. Subsequently, after default of pharmacological well-being, the ego experience again the fault, sometimes with helplessness and conscious guilt, that only the new drugs will relieve again.

It is settled in this way a vicious circle, tension depression / narcissistic omnipotence, to which the addict is "hooked". To Bergeret (1983) substances are used to combat anxiety, as a hippomanic. Another aim of the substance, for this author, is to combat the anxiety of narcissistic failure. By investing in the substance, as a true magic potion that allows them to dominate the world, drug abusers fight against the feeling of being incapable of mastering themselves.

The self-medication hypothesis posits that drug use may begin, continue or be promoted as a form of self regulation to counteract anxiety, depression, anger or feelings of subjective discomfort (Khantzian, 1985). The drug would be used not to generate well-being, but to offset discomfort. The well-being would be situation due to the avoidance of discomfort.

Psychoactive substances have been taken by the dependent to protect him against their assigned confusing or painful are the result of structural damage to his personality. According Pagés-Berthier (2002), to avoid the boom in the ego under pressure from their assigned violence emotions, drug abusers use the substance, that chains, and furious incorporation, expressing the anguish of disintegration to return for a limited time, an apparent drive to their bodily sensations. This overinvestment compulsive body by maintaining extreme sensations is the place of the object relation.

Rosa (1994), says that "as an end in itself", the drug can be used to support a daily living of anguish and emotional distress. To Bergeret (1983), the use of drugs may be a way of trying to escape the reality of the surroundings. According to this author, there is a setback for the reality principle for the pleasure principle. The personality of the drug abuser finds him limited by his emotional immaturity than by a particular psychic disturbance, remaining dependent on the pleasure principle and the imperative demands. The displeasure is so unbearable for these people as for a child. The drug abuser deprived of the reassuring object behaves like a child who sees the absent parent before having been able to acquire the concept of time, and therefore constant. So the child thinks that the match is final in itself.

According Olivenstein (1987), apparently, the pleasure supersedes drug addiction to all forms of pleasure, including sexual pleasure. This is a true regression, but this decline is not happy, because it can not be both adult and child and, although it might be, society will not tolerate. Wurmser (1987) conceptualizes drug abusers as individuals with overly harsh super-egos that, subsequently, cause conflicts. He understands drug abuse as a symptom of such underlying conflicts, motivated by narcissistic crisis. The conflict experienced by drug abusers is related with overwhelming affects which feel threatening. Hence, Wurmser (1985) advocates a multifaceted approach to treatment which includes: psychoanalytic psychotherapy, self-help groups, psychopharmacology, psychoeducation and family therapy. His psychoanalytic psychotherapy for substance abusers focuses on the substance abuser as an individual with super-ego conflicts. Treatment, therefore, involves identifying and examining the aetiology and function of one's overly harsh and stringent standards. One of the therapist tasks is to avoid colluding with the individual harsh super-ego and provide respite from such harshness through the therapy relationship. Furthermore, maintaining a strong yet warm, kind and flexible emotional presence particularly in response to relapses, impulsive behaviors and "acting out" is essential (Morgenstern & Leeds, 1993) as it models a non-punitive response to the individuals limitations. By maintaining this therapeutic frame, the individual can begin to internalize a gentles, kinder and more tolerant internal voice which strives to understand, rather than condemn, relapses and foibles that occur along the way to recover. Consequently, treating an individual with psychodynamics is facilitated by a more permissive, accepting and exploratory psychoanalytical approach which strives to modify intrapsychic structures partially by containing and examining drug abuse and failures around this use.

Khantian's model of drug abuse suggests that such individuals have particular deficits in their psychological make-up which, therefore, lead to drug abuse in order to compensate for such deficiencies (Khantzian, 1980). These deficits in their self-system which limit them from exercising self-regulatory functions such as: maintaining a healthy self-concept, regulating self-esteem and exercising appropriate self-care and self-protection. So, this approach focuses on developing self-regulatory capacities instead of conflict resolution (Morgenstern & Leeds, 1993).

Khantzian (1980) underlines the deregulation of parental caring and protective functions, leading to the incapacity of internalizing caring or protective functions, which leads, subsequently, to self-deficits. This model maintains that drug abusers tend to select drugs which will most effectively compensate for their deficits.

Khantzian and colleagues (1990) have developed a systematic approach to treatment through his Modified Dynamic Group Therapy (MDGT) approach which includes individual psychoanalytical psychotherapy, dynamic group therapy, self-help groups and a supportive, therapeutic environment for recovering drug abusers. While treatment abstinence and relapse prevention are important components, the most important focus is on characterological change and insight into alternative ways of handling the emotions and situations that lead to drug abuse. Namely, treatment revolves around addressing self deficits. Such deficits may include difficulties with affect regulation, self-esteem, interpersonal relationships and self-care (Khantzian et al., 1990).

Affect regulation includes addressing problems with affect which may include targeting the drug abuser alexithymia. Affect activation is one problem that the therapist must work to facilitate, in the actual experience, and in the expression of emotions. Affect labeling is another function which includes helping the individual to symbolize or put into words what he is feeling. Affect modulation is another skill where limits around affective expression are taught and modeled. For last, affect tolerance is developed by the therapist's emphatic, steady and containing presence in response to affects.

Interpersonal problems are another major focus in working with drug abusers and include attending to how personal deficits and drug abuse have contributed to these problems. In an interpersonal context, the patient learns to use words instead of substances to deal with his internal states.

Models of intervention based on psychoanalytic models, focus on aspects often overlooked and undervalued by other approaches. It is a journey into the interior of the people, for the way they live, feel and react to life and situations arise, eventually hypothesize the causes of psychological distress

Cognitive-Behavioral Framework for Conceptualizing Addiction

Cognitive–behavioral intervention focuses on dysfunctional patterns of thinking and behavior. During years, cognitive-behavioral therapies have been demonstrating empirical support in interventions such as motivational enhancement therapies, social skills training, stress management, relapse prevention and coping-skills training (Finney & Monahan, 1996; Miller & Brown, 1997). In most current conceptualizations of drug addiction, subjective craving is regarded as a central phenomenon, contributing to the continuation of drug use in active abusers and the occurrence of relapse in detoxified abusers (Everitt, 1997). Furthermore, cognitive factors such as memory processes, expectancies, and attentional processes are recently added to the range of cue-elicited reactivity. However, from a cognitive neuroscience point of view, cognitive processes are studied because of their mediating role between neuropsychopharmacological processes and behavior. Cognitive processes represent an essential link between stimulus, pharmacological processes, and response (Toates, 1998).

Motivational enhancement interventions are client-centered, directive approaches that enhance intrinsic motivation for behavior change. These interventions, originally developed to work with ambivalence in problem drinkers, have been widely used and tested in a broad range of health behaviors.

Patient's motivation to change is often difficult to assess, since change translates a complex, sometimes painful and complicated process. In addiction, motivation could conceptualize as a fluctuating state influenced by the environment as well as the client's cognitive and emotional weighing of the perceived harm versus benefits of drug use and of abstinence. Many of therapeutic techniques may be used to enhance clients' awareness and appreciation of the extent and severity of their substance use problems and the desirability to change. These include motivational interviewing, the use of decisional balance sheets or involvement with self-help groups.

Haaga et al., (2006) identified motivation to change in the three variables that best predict a more positive response to treatment. First, positive expectancies about treatment would lead to better outcomes. Thus, it's important to develop a good working alliance with the drug abuser in order to enhance positive expectancies. Second, greater client readiness to change predicts higher treatment success. One of the roles of the therapist is to potentiate the readiness to change. Maintaining and enhancing motivation to change are crucial therapeutic tasks. One specific factor that may contribute to readiness to change is the degree to which substance abuse has directly affected physical health, either by contributing to specific medical conditions or by complicating medical conditions with other aetiologies. The third factor related to treatment outcome is severity of drug addiction. In particular, greater severity is associated with a poorer response to treatment. Drug addiction severity predicts worse response, given that having experienced severe consequences should, in principle, increase motivation to change. However, motivation is best understood as a balance between perceived positive and negative consequences of use compared to perceived positive and negative consequences of change. Those with the most severe problems may indeed perceive many negative consequences from substance use, but they may not be able to picture clear positive consequences of abstinence if they already have irreversible medical problems, or have lost their family and occupation (Haaga et al., 2006).

When recognized the ambivalence that normally drug abusers come into treatment, therapist should adapt treatment techniques to the degree of client promptness to change. For instance, clients who are unsure if their drug addiction is a problem may respond well to an intervention that helps them consider the problems caused by their use and whether they should change, whereas they may respond negatively if pushed to make active behavior changes (Haaga et al., 2006).

Motivation is a crucial aspect of drug abuse treatment, and should consider the complexity of the person. Therapist should find a way to motivate each individual and should not have a general model that fits everyone. Therapist should help the patient to find the necessary and important reasons why he wants to go on treatment, and to recover from drug addiction.

Relapse prevention is a key aspect to be addressed in the recovery of drug abusers. As broadly reported, the causes of relapse are multifactor and sometimes unexpected, but often preventable. The unique understanding of each person will help realize the dynamics of relapse, and deepen our knowledge in this field.

By understanding the causes of relapse, the intervention model can be cast as the new information that may be key signaling what should be the path of healing and rehabilitation, given the identified risk factors.

Generally, relapse implies a recurrence of symptoms of a disease after a period of improvement or cure. Historically, the dichotomous model of disease/health considers that clients in the drug addiction field are cured or relapsed. This cross-sectional analysis of the drug addiction situation has being replaced by a longitudinal analysis in which the temporal dimension is of particular importance. Thus, abstinence versus relapse can be viewed as processes, and temporal pathways. The dynamics of these processes over time, and how they evolve is one of the basics of a psychological intervention.

Although years of clinical research, the rate of drug abuse relapse remains high. There are many related factors causing relapse in what includes ambivalence or the absence of motivation to stop drugs, presence of severe withdrawal syndrome (such as obstinate insomnia and emotional oppression), temptation by drug mates, lack of sufficient social supports, difficulty dealing with emotions, inability to deal with interpersonal conflicts, limitation of psychological defense mechanisms, inadequate coping skill, and finally, weakness to cope with negative emotions (anger, sadness, guilt) and frustration. Drug abuse relapse after abstinence is a vicious circle, which is caused by interrelated effects of many factors, such as biological, social, psychological, and environmental. Frequently, after one relapse, the confidence of overcoming drug abuse is seriously weakened.

Research on mechanisms that underlies drug addiction has shown that stress is one of the strongest predictors of relapse (Dawes et al., 2000; Kosten et al., 1986), continued drug use (Brewer et al., 1998), and increased drug craving (Sinha et al., 2000).

Drug addiction studies have exposed the importance of effective coping responses as a mediator of the effects of stress. For instance, studies have shown that positive coping skills enhancement increases the ability to manage craving and to remain abstinent despite severe stress (Brown et al., 2001; Rask et al., 2006). Alternatively, coping responses associated with negative emotions are associated with relapse (Weaver et al., 2000).

Social learning theory made an influential donation to the understanding of substance use, abuse and dependence (Bandura, 1977). General cognitive-behavioral models posit that are relevant situational cues associated with drinking and drug consumption that influence alcohol/drug related beliefs and coping strategies effectiveness. In substance abusers, these operate as situationally relapse precipitants for alcohol use or other drugs, such as nicotine, cannabis, heroin or cocaine.

Identifying patient's high-risk cues for alcohol or drug abuse plays an essential role in cognitive-behavioral models of treatment. For example, collecting information about risk situations for alcohol use could be crucial to understand patient's reasons to drink, difficulties to maintain sobriety after treatment and to generate an individually-tailored treatment program. Usually, high-risk situations that enhance the likelihood of substance use include intrapersonal events such as cognitions and emotional states, and interpersonal dimensions such as peer pressure. The pioneer and systematic work produced by Alan Marlatt and his colleagues (Marlatt & Gordon, 1985), give considerably support for an empirically-based typology of situations that present a high risk for relapse. Indeed, based on alcoholic's interviews following discharge from treatment programs, the authors demonstrated that client descriptions of their primary relapse episodes could be classified in 8 categories: Unpleasant Emotions (UE), Physical Discomfort (PD), Pleasant Emotions (PE), Testing Personal Control (TC), Urges and Temptations to Use (UT), Conflict with Others (CO), Social Pressure to Use (SP), and Pleasant Times with Others (PO).

Cognitive therapies have been developed through the pioneer work of Aaron Beck. In this paradigm, cognition is defined as the set of processes by which a person acquires information about itself and its environment, and treats them to guide their behavior.

The model proposed by Beck et al. (1993) support the idea that individuals are predisposed to drug addiction by predisposing factors that they hold, as an exaggerated sensitivity to unpleasant feelings; poor motivation to control their behavior; impulsiveness; the search for sensations and intolerance to boredom; a low frustration tolerance and, in most cases, insufficient social alternatives for pleasant sensations, with the addition of the absence of hope of obtaining it. According to Beck et al. (1993), are dysfunctional thoughts and beliefs that increase the need for drugs: in the core of the problem of the addition is a set of thoughts that seem to derive from one main thought of self-depreciation in value of their self-esteem. These central thoughts interact with the stress of everyday life to produce excessive anxiety, dysphoric mood, depression or aggression. These stressful situations not directly cause the need nor the desire for relief by drugs, but trigger thoughts related to the feeling of need to which will involve drugs. Beck et al. (1993) notes that often coexist opposing ideas about the advantages and disadvantages of taking drugs. The latter can then come to relieve the tension caused by this conflict, which of course, only adds to the maintenance of the system stress-drugs. The author points out that patient tend to minimize or deny the problems that result from proper use of drugs, or attribute these problems to causes other than the use. Some beliefs are involved in the maintenance of dependence, for example, that detoxification will cause intolerable side effects, or other well-established, that there is an inability to control the need. Indeed, Beckian cognitive psychology plan to distinguish the schemes, the overall or the steps that take place in the interactive processes ranging from information to thought and behavior.

Cognitive therapy approach intends to restrict additions to the field momentum, weakening the beliefs that feed, and, at the same time, show the patient various ways to control and modify their behavior. It is therefore an active therapy (intended to lead to action by the patient in the here and now) that should be conducted in collaboration with the patient in a structured and targeted manner.

The application of this model, which consists of changing the system of individual thought, is not limited to teaching the patient the ways to avoid or extricate themselves at risk. It must allow, with the same techniques, treating the underlying aspects of drug addiction: depression, anxiety, personality disorders, as well as all aspects of the patient's life that can contribute to potentiate stress leading to a relapse (social, interpersonal, personal, legal, marital problems).

For Haaga et al. (2006), a key component of therapy is a focus on helping the client to develop awareness of repetitive patterns of thinking and behavior that perpetuate drug addiction. Positive expectations about the effects of drugs, distorted perceptions of drinking or drug use norms in their social environment, and low self-efficacy for coping with difficult situations without alcohol or drugs exemplify patterns of thinking that may perpetuate use. Clinicians also should help clients become more aware of behavioral patterns that lead to use, such as spending time in drinking environments or with people who support and encourage use, and become more aware of the types of experiences and events that lead to use. Helping the client to develop awareness of dysfunctional patterns of thinking and behaving should be accompanied by a focus on helping the client learn alternative coping skills to manage these dysfunctional thoughts and behaviors.

The behavior effects of alcohol involve a complex interaction between biologic, pharmacologic and situational features, but also cognitive factors. Alcoholism research has been giving a particular attention to the influence of the cognitive variables on drinking decisions that maintain the excessive ingestion of alcohol and consent relapse in the alcoholic's treatment process.

The beliefs that drinkers hold about the effects of the alcohol use are referred to as alcohol expectancies. Through decades, cognitive models of addictions have been generally accepted that cognitions predict social drinking behavior. Early in the nineties, Marlatt and Rohsenow (1980) draw the attention for the important role that the expectancies about the alcohol effects played in the mediation of ingestion and behavior during acute alcohol intoxication.

Social cognitive theories recognized that alcohol use behavior is, in part, ruled by outcome expectancies connected to the perceived consequences of alcohol consumption. These expectancies are cognitive representations of alcohol correlated reinforcement. Numerous studies have been established that both negative and positive outcomes of drinking behavior are associated with alcohol consumption (Connors et al., 1988; Stacy et al., 1990; Jones &

McMahon, 1992; Oei & Baldwin 1994; Brown et al. 1998; Oei et al., 1998; Finn et al. 2000).

Drinking expectancies generally included increased social assertiveness, sexual enhancement, cognitive enhancement, tension reduction, negative affective change and dependence, and a loss of control over alcohol consumption (Young & Knight, 1989).

To our days, little research has been conducted on the reasons, motivations and other individual and social factors that influence drinking behavior among the MMT client population. As a matter of fact, normally individuals perceived their alcohol use as serving specific functions in the economy of their psychological function. For example, Hillebrand et al., (2001), study the association between alcohol effect and their specific functions among clients in methadone maintenance. The results (n = 50) confirm that drinking fulfill specific functions, with the highest prevalence's related to helping to relax (84%); stop feeling bored (68%); make yourself feel better when low or depressed (66%); forget problems (64%); help to get to sleep (54%); increase the effects of methadone or any other drug (30%); help to ''get going'' in the morning (28%); stop feeling sick in the morning (24%) and calm after using other drugs (24%).

When Spirit and Faith Address Drug Addiction: Spiritual Interventions in Addiction

It is well-known that religious practice outline a protective factor against drug consumption, above all among those who attend church regularly (Blum et al., 2003), practice the teachings of their professed religion (Hodge et al., 2001) or believe in the importance of religion in their lives (Miller et al., 2000). For instance, studies have found that spirituality negatively relates to addiction risk (Miller, 1998) and positively relates to drug abstinence (Brown et al., 2001). Higher levels of religious faith and spirituality are associated with more adaptive coping responses, higher resilience to stress, a more optimistic life orientation, greater perceived social support, and lower levels of anxiety among recovering individuals (Ellison, 1991; Kaplan et al., 1997; Kendler et al., 1997; Pardini et al., 2000). Therefore, all these statements generate some consensus in what concerns the importance of attending clients' spiritual needs during treatment and recovery (Dermatis et al., 2004), and the use of spirituality to reframe life difficulties and improve coping skills (Baetz et al., 2006).

Some authors claim that religiosity plays a role in reducing relapses among recovery drug users, suggesting that increased optimism, better perception of social support, higher resistance to stress, and reduction of stress levels would be responsible for the success of these programs (Neff et al, 2006). According to Barrett et al., (1988), this mechanism is much more closely linked to social issues, such as the re-socialization of individuals through a restructuring of their friendship circles, thus placing them in a healthier, drug-free environment.

At the present time, is already available in the substance abuse field some structured psychological interventions that increase spirituality, coping and stress reduction that should be considered by practitioners (Goeders, 2003; Laudet et al., 2006). These evidence base interventions include Mindfulness-Based Stress Reduction (Kabat-Zinn, 1982; Kabat-Zinn et al., 1997; Miller et al., 1995), Spiritual Self Schema Therapy (Avants et al., 2001; Margolin et al., 2006) and Mindfulness-Based Relapse Prevention (Marlatt et al., 2004; Witkiewitz et al., 2005).

An adaptation of the Mindfulness-Based Stress Reduction Program by Kabat-Zinn (1982), that focused on relapse prevention, is a group-based intervention, that teaches participants practices such as the body scan; awareness of breathing, sitting, walking and eating meditation; gentle stretching and mindful yoga; didactic information about healthy and unhealthy responses to stress; and group dialogue.

An additional model of intervention is Spirituality in Recovery (Amaro et al., 2004a), a group curriculum that teaches participants how to integrate spiritual resources in the context of drug addiction programs. The sessions are intended to facilitate ways to discover and practice spirituality freed of theological arguments or religious discourse. The main goal of this curriculum is to enable participants to create a self-defined spirituality in the context of their road towards recovery.

Another form of recovery is The Women's HIV Prevention Leadership Training Institute based on a curriculum (Amaro et al., 2004b) that integrates HIV prevention based on work by El-Bassell & Schilling (1992). This enhancement provides information on AIDS transmission and prevention, condom use, assertiveness training, problem solving, and communication skills.

Spirituality is a coping mechanism to consider in addressing drug addiction. Many of these individuals have lost all connection with life, because they deteriorated many important areas of their life: personal, interpersonal relationships, family and social relationships, and at work. Religion is always an important anchor in society, there are always doors open for those who are suffering, whether what nature it presents. In this sense, faith can be instrumental in helping these individuals in their recovery, providing them with a new coping mechanism, which may be decisive in desperate moments, based on social support of the religious community.

CONCLUSIONS

Drug addiction represents, above all, a "way of being in this world". Addiction is not a simple behavior, but rather a general attitude in the face of existence that implies a whole way of life. In psychotherapeutic context, the therapist should support a correction of the relationship with the world, away from the pathological drug experience, that usually represents an advantaged and disadvantaged way of life that restores a perfect harmony with the external and internal world.

Often, drug and alcohol consumption masks internal conflicts that cause painful unrest to patients. In these cases, therapists should pay cautious attention to problems beyond the "main" problem of drug addiction, as emotional, psychological or psychiatric disturbances. Indeed, psychological models has been pointing out the importance of not approaching addictive behaviors as a mere symptomatic expression of intrapsychic faults or personality disorders, since this may lead to unfocused and sometimes incessant treatment processes. Therefore, attention has been draw to the psychosocial context of substance consumption, in which addicted behavior occurs in relation to situational and environmental circumstances, beliefs and expectations or craving. Contextual factors are important to understand substance use disorders, given that drug use and abuse "exist in a complex web of social forces" (Moos, 2003). Treatment represents one of many forces with an impact on someone who is trying to reduce or give up drugs or alcohol; nevertheless, it could not be an enduring or significant long-term force unless it includes a careful attention to the reshaping of the social environment. According to Gossop (1996), treatments should be focused on different and compatible goals, such as the reduction of psychosocial problems, directly and not-directly related to the drug problem, and the reduction of risk behaviors associated with the use of drugs. Nevertheless, psychosocial interventions in addictive patients should be given carefully, mainly if patients present a multifaceted polysubstance abuse pattern and therapists did not delineate a more personalized therapeutic program.

Each person who comes with an addiction problem has a unique profile with its capabilities, shortcomings and limitations. Definitely, a psychological intervention for drug addiction is a challenge to the mentality and resilience of the therapist, which has to be flexible, creative and have confidence in his work and never put aside his foremost purpose with a patient: firstly, do not harm. As Moos (2005) posits, psychological health-care providers intend to ease the pain of individuals in distress and help them overcome their substance use and mental problems. Though, if we believe that treatment has curative power and contributes to patients' improvement, we must consider the thought that, at times, treatment also may have iatrogenic effects and contribute to patients' deterioration.

Chapter 9

9. COGNITIVE-BEHAVIORAL INDICATORS OF ALCOHOLISM PHENOTYPES IN PATIENTS IN OPIOID MAINTENANCE TREATMENT: AN EMPIRICAL ANALYSIS

ABSTRACT

Polydrug use is common among patients in opioid maintenance programs. Heroin users often abuse alcohol, which may deteriorate the outcome of opioid maintenance treatment.

Excessive alcohol consumption among opioid maintenance patients has been associated with quality of life impairments and with serious social and health costs. Patients who are dependent both on illicit drugs and alcohol may have a poorer treatment outcome than patients without alcohol problems. The clinical and psychosocial treatment of these patients presents challenging work for the clinician. Therefore, treatment outcomes may be further improved if clinical subtypes of substance abusers could be identified and matched to an adequate treatment program.

In this study we aim to assess the prevalence of a drinking problem and analyze the cognitive and behavioral features of problematic alcohol use in opioid addicts according to Cloninger and Lesch's alcoholism typologies in a sample of 102 heroin-dependent patients in Opioid Maintenance Treatment. This sample was selected in the Addiction Unit of the Psychiatric Service of Santa Maria University Hospital, in Lisbon-Portugal.

Results show that alcohol use and alcohol-related problems are frequent among heroin-dependent patients. Study clinical descriptors discriminate Cloninger's type I and type II drinking problem and confirm this binary alcoholism classification in this population. Heroin-dependent patients classified as Cloninger´s type II problem drinkers showed a more severe cognitive-behavior profile than those with a type I alcohol problem, concerning alcohol-taking situation prototypes, beliefs and expectancies about alcohol effects. Data only allows preliminary results about the Lesch's alcoholism classification

This cognitive and behavioral multidimensional assessment has relevant indicators to diagnose different drinking problems among the opioid maintenance programs population. It may improve intervention and treatment outcomes, reducing current health and psychosocial damage associated with an alcohol-abusing lifestyle.

Keywords: Cognitive-behavioral; alcoholism; phenotypes; opioid maintenance treatment.

Opioid Maintenance Treatment (OMT) with methadone or buprenorphine is a broadly used form of substitute therapy, with effective results in heroin dependence trials (West et al., 2000; Stein et al., 2005; Soyka et al. 2008; Costa et al., 2008). Studies demonstrate that it retains patients in treatment, decreases heroin use and related crime and health problems (Bertschy, 1995; Mattick et al., 2003). Even so, in some cases treatment discharge is a common reality. Treatment discontinuation or dropouts seems to be associated with loss of contact with treatment services, non-compliance with program rules, death or other medical problems, transfer to another program and achievement of goals (Magura et al., 1998). In order to improve retention and to identify risk or dropout, treatment enhancement efforts should focus on patient motivation, therapeutic involvement and frequency of session attendance, and also on the therapist perceptions (Simpson et al., 1997). According to our experience, the attendance at a weekly psychotherapeutic group could help to sustain different emotional problems habitually associated with motivation to change, dropout or relapse.

Treating OMT patients with combined heroin, cocaine and alcohol problems is more challenging than working with clients with less opioid polydrug use (Rowan-Szal et al., 2000).

The aim of the study is to (1) screen problematic alcohol use in opiate addicts in maintenance treatment; (2) assess cognitive-behavioral key constructs of drinking such as craving, alcohol related beliefs and expectancies and high-risk situations; (3) measure how alcoholism typologies behave in opiate addicts with an alcohol problem and (4) assess these previous cognitive-behavioral key constructs of drinking across alcoholism subtypes.

METHODS AND MEASURES

The sample comprised 102 heroin-dependent patients, admitted in the Addiction Unit of the Psychiatric Service of Santa Maria University Hospital in Lisbon, Portugal.

During the outpatient therapeutical programme clinical and socio-demographic information was collected with a brief standardized interview. After that, the patients fulfill the Michigan Alcoholism Screening Test (MAST). In the second moment, only patients who score positive in the screening procedure (MAST positive) were eligible for the study. As a result, patients complete the Inventory of Drug Taking Situations adapted for alcohol (IDTS), the Alcohol Related Beliefs and Expectations Questionnaire (ABEQ), the Penn Alcohol Craving Scale (PACS) and the substance abuse and dependence disorders section of the Mini International Neuropsychiatric Interview (MINI). The MINI is a short, structured diagnostic interview for DSM-IV and ICD-10 psychiatric disorders, which takes approximately 15 minutes to administer. Patients were administered with the MINI to assess the presence of lifetime DSM-IV diagnoses of alcohol and drug use disorders.

The Alcohol Personal Beliefs and Expectancies Inventory (APBEI) is self-administered instrument constitute by 61 items, design to evaluate beliefs and expectancies related to alcohol effect. To each belief there are five categories of a possible answer (Likert type), from "I don't agree" to "I completely agree". The APBEI has demonstrated good characteristics of reliability and validity in alcohol user populations. The inventory reaches good psychometric properties with highly intern consistency: correlation coefficient was 0.973 to (Split-half), the Spearman-Brown coefficient was equal to 0.986 and the alpha Cronbach was equal to 0.984. Temporal stability was adequate with a Spearman coefficient of correlation equal to 0.764. Factorial analysis isolate 6 factors, that explain 62.62% of the total variance: (F1) Factor 1: Global Positive Effects and Facilitation of Social Interactions; (F2) Factor 2: Expectancies on Activation and Sexual Pleasure effects; (F3) Factor 3: Composed by items that translate expectancies on Positive Effects in Activity and Humour; (F4) Factor 4: Dimension of the expectancies of alcohol might work as Escape to Negative Emotional States; (F5) Factor 5: Translate expectancies of Sexual Disinhibition; and (F6) Factor 6: Express expectancies on alcohol related to Diminution of Negative Feelings about himself and of Evaluated Anxiety. A global result that corresponds to the total of all answers is also obtained This tool may be useful in several contexts, like in clinical practice with alcoholics or individuals with drinking problems, since it allows the operationalization of cognitive variables that are considered to influence behavior decisions as drinking (Gouveia et al., 1993).

Alcohol craving is considered one of the core components of the cognitive-behavioral model of alcoholism and a strong predictor of relapse. Craving was assessed with the PACS (Flannery et al., 1999). This instrument is a 5-item self-administered scale designed to assess the alcohol craving severity (frequency, intensity, duration, resistance, and overall craving) during the previous week. In an alcoholic Portuguese outpatient population, the PACS have revealed good psychometric qualities (Pombo et al., *in press*).

Quantity-Frequency (QF) method was used in order to estimate the average number of drinking days over a certain period (typical week) and then to estimate the average number of drinks consumed per drinking day. The QF drinking variable was then calculated as the product result of those measures (in standard drinks) - average number of drinks per week. A standard drink was defined as one beer, one glass of wine, one glass or shot of liquor.

All subjects were evaluated in a face-to-face interview and asked directly about the items that comprise the operationalized criteria described by each alcoholism typology. Here we provide an overview of the clinical criteria and decision process for subtyping the Cloninger approach and the Lesch alcoholic typology. Patients subtype allocation for Cloninger et al. (1981) model follows the von Knorring et al. (1985) criteria. For type I were the presences of subjective drinking problems start after age 25, first treatment contact after age 30 and few social complications (legal, work problems). Type II included subjective drinking problems start before age 25, first treatment contact before age 30 and frequent social complications (legal, work problems). Decision procedure in the set was: when the specified criteria of each subtype (I or II) was present, subjects received a positive score in each item endorsed (+1), and, when the specified criteria was not in attendance, subjects received a negative score (-1). Afterwards, for patient's allocation purposes, algebraic sum of the items are performed and the quantitative scores were transformed into categorical data on the basis of higher total positive scores (or less negative) in each subtype. Sums equal to 0 were considered to be undiagnosed classification.

The classification procedure of the 4 alcoholism sub-types of Lesch et al. (1988) was based in a computerized Decision Tree. This PC-guided version of patient's allocation (Decision Tree) is nowadays available in computer software in most European languages, including Portuguese, and it has already been used in various international trials (Lesch et al., 2001; Hillmacher et al., 2006; Walter et al., 2006; Pombo et al., 2007; 2009). The descriptors for each type are as follow: Type I: social drinking develops to habitual drinking, medium abstinence syndrome occurs early, craving, positive family history for alcoholism and minimal social effects; Type II: alcohol consumption as a coping strategy against anxiety, suicidal intentions (mainly under the influence of alcohol) and no severe somatic alcohol related disorders or withdrawal; Type III: alcohol consumption as a form of self treatment (depression, sleep disorders), suicidal tendencies, psychiatric co-morbidity, aggressive behavior even without alcohol and mild somatic withdrawal; and Type IV: cerebral disturbances or prenatal damage before the termination of brain development, grand mal seizures (not only during withdrawal), enuresis nocturnal, deterioration of individual's psychic, organic and social sphere.

All researchers that performed the subtyping procedure enclose clinical skills to assess addiction patients and scientific knowledge to manage the principles of each classification system.

In order to accurately identify drugs consumption in our sample; all patients were urine tested for the presence of heroin, cocaine and cannabis metabolites. The urine analysis procedure was performed by staff nurses of our Addiction Unit.

All subjects were informed about the study and given the consent for participation.

The exclusion criteria were: presence of serious physical disease, severe psychiatric disorder (schizophrenia and other psychotic disorders, dementia, delirium), state of alcoholic intoxication during assessment and marked cognitive deficit.

Statistical Analysis

Considering normally distributed data (Kolmogorov-Smirnov test) parametric methods were used to calculate numerical relations between data. Chi-square (2-vs-2), student's t test and ANOVA comparisons were used to study the relation between groups. Pearson correlational analysis technique was used to measure the strength of a supposed linear association between the variables. Statistical analysis was performed with Statistical Package for

Social Sciences (SPSS-Version 12.0). Statistical significance was defined at $p < 0.05$.

RESULTS

The sample comprised 102 opiate dependent patients, being 79.4% males (N=81) and 20.6% females (N=21). Age varied between 27 and 53 years, with a mean value of 41.5 years (SD = 6.7). Females (mean age =36.8 years) were significantly ($p<0.01$) younger than males (mean age = 42.7 years). The sample was entirely Caucasian (100%). Regarding marital status, 16.6 % were married, 61.8 % were single, and 20.6% were separated. Education ranged between 2 and 15 years, with a mean value of 7.2 years of school attendance (SD=2.8). Concerning occupational status, 33.3 % were active workers, 8.8 % were already retired and 57.8% were unemployed. No other significant differences ($p >0.05$) were found between genders and the socio-demographic features.

In what is considered maintenance for the treatment of heroin-dependent outpatients, 58.4% are allocated in the methadone subgroup, with daily mean dosages of 65.1 mg (SD=22.7); and 41.6% are allocated in the buprenorphine group, with daily mean dosages of 7.4 mg (SD=2.4). The patients report a mean of 20.4 (SD=32.0) months of heroin abstinence.

Urine analysis showed that 14.6% of the patients score positive for opiate metabolites, 19.5% score positive for cocaine metabolites, and 52.4% score positive for cannabis metabolites (THC).

Of 102 patients enrolled, 45.1% (N=46) have *positive MAST scores* (greater than 7), indicating putative *alcohol related problems.* Socio-demographic characterization of this sample indicates that, 83.7% were males and 16.3% were females; 12.3 % were married, 65.3 % were single, and 22.4% were separated; education level has a mean value of 6.5 years of school attendance; 28.6 % were active workers, 16.3 % were already retired and 55.1% were unemployed. No significant differences ($p >0.05$) were found between populations with MAST positive and negative cut-point scores.

Concerning clinical characterization of the problematic alcohol use sample, data shows that the average age of drinking onset was 13.7 (SD=7.5), age of alcohol abuse onset was 13.8 (SD=3.6) and the age of alcohol dependence onset was 28.7 years (SD=6.1). Subjects reported an average number of drinks per week (QF) of 72.1 units (SD=62.0).

History of family alcoholism was positive in 47.9% of the cases, being 39.6% with a father or a mother (2.1%) with an alcohol problem and 2.1% with a grandmother or grandfather (12.5%).

Of the total sample, 39.2% had a lifetime diagnosis of alcohol dependence according to the criteria of DSM-IV (MINI diagnostic interview).

After the alcoholism screening, patients were subtyped according to the following classifications sets. The decision tree system of Lesch typology classified the alcohol dependents in the following way: 33.3 % as type II; 40.0 % as type III and 26.7 % as type IV. Dicothomic typology of Cloninger with the operationalized criteria derived from von Knorring et al. showed that 67.4% of individuals were classified as type I and 32.6% as type II. The IDTS eight subscales profile and second order global categories showed the following mean scores: (UE) Unpleasant Emotions (9.8; SD=8.0); (PD) Physical Discomfort (3.2; SD=3.3), (PE) Pleasant Emotions (6.4; SD=4.3); (TC) Testing Personal Control (3.2; SD=3.1), (UT) Urges and Temptations to Use (3.4; SD=3.7); (CO) Conflict with Others (7.8; SD=7.3); (SO) Social Pressure to Use (3.8; SD=3.9); (PT) Pleasant Times with Others (4.6; SD= 4.4); 1. Negative situations (20.9; SD=18.4); 2. Positive situations (10.9; SD=8.8) and 3. Temptation situations (10.5; SD=10.8). Concerning APBEI, the mean scores for the factors are as follow: F1; mean equal to 60.4; SD=26.8; F2; mean equal to 22.3; SD=10.9; F3; mean equal to 32.5; SD=15.8; F4; mean equal to 27.8; SD=17.6; F5; mean equal to 7.1; SD=3.5; and F6; mean equal to 23.7; SD=16.8. The mean total score for the PACS was 5.6 (SD=6.6).

No significant relationships were found between alcohol related variables (MAST, QF, age onset) and maintenance treatment variables such as buprenorphine or methadone daily mean dosages and drug screening in urine analyses.

PACS total score significantly correlate positive with the following subscales of the IDTS: UE ($r = 0.30$*); PE. ($r = 0.44$**), CO. ($r = 0.40$**); SP. ($r = 0.45$**) and PT. ($r = 0.51$**). No significant correlations were found between APBEI and the PACS. Significant positive correlations were observed between the MAST total score and the IDTS subscales UE. ($r = 0.40$ **); UT. ($r = 0.37$*) and CO. ($r = 0.45$**). MAST total score also correlate with the factors F2. ($r = 0.33$*); F4. ($r = 0.45$**); F6. ($r = 0.46$**) and total score ($r = 0.33$*) of the APBEI. No significant correlations were established between the APBEI, PACS and IDTS and socio-demographic features such as age or education level. Several significant positive correlations were found between the APBEI and the IDTS in the heroin-dependent population with concomitant problem drinking. Table 1 shows the matrix correlations between IDTS and the APBEI scores.

Table 8. matrix correlations between IDTS and the APBEI scores

PABEQ	F1	F2	F3	F4	F5	F6	T
IDTS							
UE	.52**	.55**	.61**	.25	.53**	.25	.55**
PD	.38*	.48**	.47**	.18	.46**	.21	.43**
PE	.36**	.52**	.50**	.13	.60**	.40	.40**
TC	.42**	.48**	.44**	.16	.46**	.23	.43**
UT	.55**	.68**	.57**	.52**	.60**	.51**	.67**
CO	.67**	.70**	.74**	.38**	.60**	.31**	.70**
SO	.42**	.64**	.47**	.23	.57**	.23	.48**
PT	.54**	.76**	.60**	.24	.68**	.19	.58**

** $p<0.01$; * $p<0.05$.

Taking into account the Cloninger et al., (1981) classification, the statistical comparative procedure disclosed the following results: Heroin-dependent patients classified as type II problem drinkers showed significative ($t=-2.6$; $p<.05$) higher scores in MAST (MAST total score equal to 18.1), when comparing to Heroin-dependent patients classified as type I problem drinkers (MAST total score equal to 12.1); Heroin-dependent patients classified as type II problem drinkers, started to abuse and depend on alcohol ($t=4.1$, $t=4.5$, respectively; $p<.01$) earlier (mean ages of 18.3 and 24.0 years, respectively), than Heroin-dependent patients classified as type I problem drinkers (mean ages of 24.6 and 32.6 years, respectively); Heroin-dependent patients classified as type II problem drinkers, reported significative ($t=-2.6$; $p<.05$) higher average number of drinks per week (QF equal to 106.7 units), when comparing to Heroin-dependent patients classified as type I problem drinkers (QF equal to 57.1 units).

For IDTS comparisons in type I and type II patients, total scores were used. Hence, heroin-dependent patients classified as type II problem drinkers showed significative higher scores in UE, PD, TC, UT, CO, N and T, when comparing to heroin-dependent patients classified as type I problem drinkers. Table 2 shows the IDTS scores according to Cloninger typology of alcoholism in heroin-dependent patients.

Regarding APBEI comparisons in type I and type II patients, results showed that heroin-dependent patients classified as type II problem drinkers showed significative ($p<0.05$) higher scores in positive F1; F3 and total score, when comparing to heroin-dependent patients classified as type I problem drinkers. Table 3 shows the APBEI scores according to Cloninger typology of alcoholism in heroin-dependent patients.

Table 9. IDTS scores according to Cloninger typology of alcoholism in heroin-dependent patients

Cloninger Set vs. IDTS	Type I X	(SD)	Type II X (SD)	t test	p
UE. unpleasant emotions	7.0	(6.5)	15.6	(7.5) -3.8	0.01
PD. physical discomfort	2.3	(2.8)	4.9	(4.4) -2.1	0.05
PE. pleasant emotions	6.4	(3.2)	6.7	(4.0)	ns
TC. testing personal control	2.4	(2.3)	4.8	(4.6) -2.0	0.05
UT. urges and temptations	2.6	(2.7)	5.2	(4.6) -2.2	0.05
CO. conflict with others	4.4	(5.0)	14.4	(8.4) -4.8	0.01
SO. social pressure to use	3.3	(3.9)	5.0	(5.5)	ns
PT. pleasant times with others	4.0	(3.9)	5.8	(5.2)	ns
N. Negative situations	13.8	(12.3)	34.9	(18.8) -.4.3	0.01
P. Positive situations	10.4	(7.4)	12.6	(8.6)	ns
T. Temptation situations	8.4	(7.8)	15.0	(14.1) -1.9	0.05

Table 10. APBEI scores according to Cloninger typology of alcoholism in heroin-dependent patients

	Type I		Type II t test		p	
Cloninger Set vs. APBEI	X	(SD)	X (SD)			
F1.	52.9	(21.8)	75.8	(27.2)	-2.9	0.05
F2.	20.3	(8.3)	26.5	(13.9)		ns
F3.	27.1	(11.1)	42.9	(17.8)	-3.5	0.01
F4.	25.6	(20.2)	32.8	(11.8)		ns
F5.	6.7	(3.4)	8.0	(3.7)		ns
F6.	21.5	(19.5)	28.6	(10.1)		ns
Total score	122.7	(47.4)	172.3	(61.8)	-2.8	0.05

No significant differences ($p > 0.05$) were found between Cloninger subtypes and socio-demographic variables or others such as PACS, methadone or buprenorphine dosages, alcoholism family history or drug screening in urine analyses.

Lesch alcoholism classification in heroin dependent patients did not showed significant differences regarding APBEI, IDST and PACS; whereas we found a marginal statistical difference ($p < 0.06$) related to the subscale CO of IDTS, in what type IV patients showed higher scores (mean equal to 12.5; SD=7.0), when comparing to type II patients (mean equal to 5.3; SD=7.7). We also observe a tendency to report higher scores in APBEI and IDST in type IV and type III patients, when comparing to type II patients, however, none of these differences were significant ($p>0.05$).

Discussion

Polysubstance use is an unequivocal realism in modern addictions, been the simultaneous use of alcohol in heroin-dependent populations one of the most frequently and problematic behavior, since the alcohol problem often may remain hidden behind a more prominent illegal drug problem. This concern evidently augments when studies reported the considerable lack of treatment for alcohol related problems that occur among patients in opiate maintenance (El-Bassel et al., 1993).

Like in quite a few studies, the frequency of alcohol related problems in opioid addiction populations was high (Backmund et al., 2003; Rittmannsberger et al., 2000; Dobler-Mikola et al., 2005; Hillebrand et al., 2001; Senbanjo et al., 2006; Stenbacka et al., 2007). The alcohol abuse measurement procedure in our heroin-dependent population undergoing OMT, reached a high prevalence of problem drinking, whether this was achieved by a screening method as MAST cut-point score, or according to the diagnostic criteria of DSM-IV (substance abuse section of MINI). Definitely, alcohol use and alcohol-related problems was confirmed to be common among heroin-dependent patients, in what about half of the patients showed indications of problem drinking and approximately one third meet the lifetime diagnosis of alcohol dependence (Maddux and Elliot, 1975; Joseph and Appel, 1985; Ottomanelli, 1999; El-Bassel et al., 1993; Hillebrand et al., 2001; Stenbacka et al., 2007). Several studies highlight the importance of screening alcohol problems in order to prevent the major impact of his recurrent related-problems, especially if heavy drinking continued to remain undetected in the treatment setting. For example, opioid addicted individuals who abused alcohol had a longer arrest history, higher rate of mortality, greater involvement in secondary abuse of other drugs, more severe psychopathology in childhood, a larger prevalence's of antisocial or borderline personality disorders diagnoses, greater global impairment and are at greater risk of drug overdose (Rounsaville et al. 1982; Joseph and Appel, 1985; Roszell et al., 1986; El-Bassel et al., 1993; Chatham et al., 1995; Best et al., 1999). In addition, an alcohol abusing lifestyle could be particularly dangerous to exposure to HIV duo to the influence of alcohol effect. Certainly, patients who consume alcohol and illicit drugs have a higher probability of risk behaviors and subsequent HIV infection (Ottomanelli, 1992). Patients who drink heavily and participate in an OMT may also be at risk of combined Central Nervous System (CNS) depressant pharmacological effects of both substances. For instance, patients could drink to increase the effects of methadone. However, in this study there was no significant correlation between alcohol-related variables and methadone or buprenorphine dosages, which is not consistent with studies stating that MMT patients with associated excessive alcohol use may need higher methadone dosages (Ottomanelli, 1999) and that additional heroin and alcohol use can be reduced by higher methadone dosages (Hartel et al., 1995; Maxwell and Shinderman, 1999).

We also did not find any relationship between the alcohol-related variables and the drug screening in urine analyses, suggesting that alcohol-related problems was not associated with more illicit drug use, a result contrary to others reviews, that reported a positive association between alcohol use and relapse into illicit drugs (Stenbacka et al., 2007). They underlined as well that alcohol dependence can deteriorate the outcome of methadone treatment (Gossop et al., 2006; Ottomanelli, 1999).

It may be put forward that many opiate dependent individuals report the frequent use of alcohol to cope with psychological discomfort related to heroin addiction rehabilitation. Ottomanelli, (1999) points out that alcohol abuse appeared to be more directly related to biological variables (i.e., potentiator of other drugs, relaxant) and to psychological variables (i.e., stimulus to socialization, and psychopathology), which enhanced the conclusion that alcohol abuse by methadone patients is as much a function of the lifestyle of the addicted individual as a biological need to alleviate withdrawal distress.

As in previous studies focused in alcohol dependent populations, the subtype distribution prevalence's have distinguished the predominance of Cloninger´s type I patients (2/3 patients), and Lesch´s type II and III (Bleich et al. 2004; Carpenter and Hasin, 2001; Hillmacher et al., 2006; Lykouras et al. 1994; Pombo et al., 2007; Pombo and Lesch, 2009). Recently, a closer examination of patients' classification relationship between Lesch et al. subtypes and Cloninger et al. model found a moderate overlap between Lesch et al. type IV and von Knorring et al criteria of Cloninger Type II. The authors mention that these results may be explained by the overlap of some of the operationalized criteria used to define each alcoholic subtype (Pombo and Lesch, 2009).

Approaching the alcoholic subtypes classification on a basis of a spectrum of severity, Cloninger type I and Lesch type II and III should be considered as a moderate severity subgroup and Cloninger type II and Lesch type VI as a high severity subgroup (Pombo and Lesch, 2009).

Craving can be defined as a strong desire/urge towards alcohol consumption. In the study analysis, PACS positively correlated with some subscales of the IDTS, which means that the heroin-dependent population with a drinking problem who reports more alcohol-related craving in the most recent week, tend to generally identify triggers to use alcohol associated with pleasant times with others, social pressure to use, conflict with others, pleasant and unpleasant emotions. These results suggested that alcohol craving is a regular associate of alcohol use emotional triggers. In some extent, these findings go in accordance with previous studies who found that alcohol dependent "cravers" showed significantly higher scores in negative emotions (Rubonis et al., 1994; Cooney et al., 1997; Litt et al., 2000; Andersohn and Kiefer; 2004) as depression, anxiety or aggressivity, supporting the concept of negative and positive craving - cognitive component of craving induced by negative and positive emotions (Pombo et al., *in press*). Contrary to expected, the PACS did not correlate with the Urges and Temptations to Use subscale of IDTS.

Concerning the Cloninger et al., (1981) classification, heroin-dependent patients classified as type II problem drinkers showed more alcohol-related problems, started to abuse and depend on alcohol earlier and reported higher average number of drinks per week, when comparing to heroin-dependent patients classified as type I problem drinkers. These results from the clinical profile of the sample clearly discriminate the type I and type II Cloninger´s *et al.* (1981) approach and visibly validate this binary alcoholism classification in an opioid addiction population with concomitant alcohol abuse problem. According to this classification, type I patients, recognized as low-severity/vulnerability subgroup, are characterized by showing a later onset of the drinking problem and less alcohol related problems, and type II patients, acknowledged as high-severity/vulnerability subgroup, by an early onset of the drinking problem, family history of alcoholism problems, antecedents of psychopathology and severe alcohol related problems (Babor and Caetano, 2006).

Back in 1985, Marlatt and Gordon developed an empirical eight-category of excessive drinking situations based on the circumstances that surround the after-treatment relapse episode of the alcoholics. Comprehensive evaluations of relapse situations have been demonstrating negative situation triggers with a fundamental role in the alcohol consume (type II re)engagement. For example, the study of Marlatt and Gordon (1985) concluded that in 35% of the cases the relapses occur by triggers related to negative emotions, 16% interpersonal conflicts with others and 20% by social pressure. Another study concluded that 62–73% of relapse episodes are related to negative emotions and social pressure (Lowman et al., 1996). On the grounds of this work, cognitive and behavioral relapse prevention programs for the psychological treatment of addictions focus on training clients in identifying and coping with their own high-risk situations for heavy drinking. This intervention might be assist with the fulfillment of a psychometric tool as the IDTS that offers a broad profile of the situations in which a client has used alcohol in the past year. Certainly, according to Turner et al., (1997), the implementation of IDTS as a treatment planning tool in clinical practice offers the therapist an effortlessly administered aid to the detection of a patient's high-risk situations for use of a particular drug.

One of the main aims of this research was to assess how the cognitive-behavioral taxonomy of excessive drinking situations could respond to the dichotomic classification of alcohol abuse of Cloninger. So, when considering alcohol use triggers assessed by the scores of IDTS taxonomy, results showed that heroin-dependent patients classified as type II problem drinkers were significantly more likely to abuse on alcohol in situations related to UE, PD, TC, UT, CO, N and T, than those classified as heroin-dependent patients classified as type I problem drinkers. In general, heroin-dependent patients classified as type II problem drinkers reported a more severe alcohol-taking profile than those with type I alcohol problem. This fact goes in conformity with previous studies that found that high negative profile patients have elevated alcohol dependence scores (Annis and Graham, 1995; Turner et al., 1997). Nevertheless, with further examination we could observe that heroin-dependent patients classified as type II problem drinkers were much more vulnerable to negative situation triggers like intrapsychic unpleasant emotions (e.g. anger, anxiety, depression) or interpersonal conflituality (e.g.., discussions with others), than heroin-dependent patients classified as type I problem drinkers. These results are consistent with Waldrop et al., (2007), who compared high-risk triggers and situations among persons with alcohol dependence or cocaine dependence, with or without posttraumatic stress disorder (PTSD). The authors observe that individuals with PTSD+ reported significantly greater substance use in response to negative situations, as compared to PTSD− individuals, supporting this finding with the self-medication theory, in which subjects who experience high rates of negative situations use substances in an attempt to minimize such symptoms. In line with this construction, that enhances the negative reward properties of alcohol, our current findings regarding alcohol use situational triggers and the Cloninger typology might be explain by the high severity profile of disease that typically characterized type II patients, notable by an early onset and frequent psychiatric comorbidity (Babor and Caetano, 2006; Pombo and Lesch, 2009).

These two different IDTS profiles identified from type I/II patients may prove to be suitable for research analysis, but also of greater relevance for clinical intervention within a cognitive-behavioral perspective. Indeed, from a cognitive and behavioral psychological standpoint, we may suggest the development of intervention strategies designed to increase patient's coping self-efficacy, in order to improve perceived internal control over alcohol use. This proposal should have particular focus in type II individuals, since they present a higher severity profile, particular vulnerable to negative situation triggers (e.g. anxiety, social pressure) and research indicates that the greater the level of alcohol dependence, the lower the confidence in the ability to resist the urge to drink heavily in high-risk situations, especially in situations involving unpleasant emotions and conflict with others (Sklar et al., 1997). For these patients, programmes that encourage stress management and social skills training may be essential. In the future we should afford empirical support for the hypothesis that type II patients present a lack of perceived control over alcohol use and a lower confidence in the ability to resist drinking heavily in high-risk situations.

Expectancies usually result form the drinker previous direct and indirect learning experiences with alcohol, and are presumed to be central in decisions to drink (Connors et al., 1988). Generally, drinkers were able to identify quite a few areas of alcohol effects. For example, reduction of negative emotional states, global positive effect, sexual activation, tension reduction, social anxiety reduction, or decreased loneliness and boredom. Almost certainly, drinkers may be more susceptible to use alcohol if they enclose the belief that the alcohol ingestion is an efficient way of dealing with the own negative emotions and facilitate a more affirmative social behavior. All these expectancies are thought to operate in decision making processes and are hypothesized to have a prevailing independently effect on drinking behaviors. A broad evaluation of personal expectancies about the alcohol effect provides to the clinician a better understanding of the cognitive dimension of patient's decisions to drink and also allows a more accurate elaboration of therapeutic programs, mostly in populations with polysubstance use. In methadone maintenance patients, alcohol is predominantly used to fulfill specific functions as helping to relax; stop feeling bored; make yourself feel better when low or depressed; forget problems; help to get to sleep; increase the effects of methadone or any other drug; help to ''get going'' in the morning; stop feeling sick in the morning and calm after using other drugs.

As expected, APBEI discriminate individuals with different levels of problem drinking. Study revealed that heroin-dependent patients classified as type II problem drinkers endorse generally higher levels of alcohol related-expectancies, especially about positive global effects and social interaction facilitation and positive effects on activation and humor, when comparing to heroin-dependent patients classified as type I problem drinkers. This finding goes in accordance with numerous studies, who concluded that individuals who drink more and present a higher problem drinking severity have significantly more positive expectancies about the alcohol effects, which will result in desirable outcomes who promote the increase of alcohol use (Brown et al., 1985; Connors *et al.,* 1988; Stacy et al., 1990; Oei and Baldwin 1994; Brown et al. 1998; Oei et al., 1998; Finn et al. 2000).

Even though, it's important to question why type II patients, acknowledged to exhibit and recognized more alcohol related consequences, report higher levels of expectancies related to the putative alcohol effect when they face up higher levels of negative outcome effects. It seems that the behavioral and social consequences related to alcohol abuse did not influence as much alcohol related cognitions in type II problem drinkers. Self-medication hypothesis might attempt to explain this conception, given the fact that patients who experience more psychological distress, like type II patients (high-severity/vulnerability subgroup), may achieve more reward properties derived from the ability of alcohol play down such negative feelings and symptoms. Other alternative explanation implicates a particular cluster of personality traits that generally characterized type II patients – high novelty seeking and low harm avoidance. These traits reflecting impulsivity and desinhibition may account to a greater exploration of the environment and also make type II patients more vulnerable to pharmacological benefits of alcohol, which could enhance alcohol related cognitions.

These assertions recognized that cognitions could also account to sustain the higher prevalence's of alcohol related problems in type II patients. Indeed, the combination of positive cognitions related to alcohol effect with impulsivity, a poor inhibitory control quality that noticeably characterized Cloninger type II problem drinker's profile, could explain why these patients have difficulties in restrain problematic drinking and present a poorer prognosis.

Cognitions might predict alcohol use in several drinking situations. In fact, expectancies reported by alcohol users more often deal with intrapersonal and interpersonal conflicts in social situations (Connors et al., 1988). As predicted, APBEI positive correlates with IDTS subscales, with the significant coefficients ranging from a low 0.31 (APBEI total score vs. CO subscale of IDTS) to a high 0.74 (APBEI F4 vs. CO subscale of IDTS). These findings clearly suggest that patients who endorse more general positive beliefs and expectancies related to alcohol effect tend to drank heavily across more intra-inter personal situations. We may consider that in high risk-situations for alcohol use, beliefs and expectancies related to alcohol effect become more prominent, rising the vulnerability for drinking behavior. As Connors et al. (1988) mention, "if an adequate coping response is not available or not emitted, there results a decreased sense of self-efficacy and concomitant positive outcome expectancies regarding alcohol, which taken together lead to an increased probability that the alcoholic will drink in that situation". In a study related to drinking outcome expectancies during relapse situations among male alcoholics, the authors reported that almost half of the expectancies reported dealt with drinking as an aid in coping with a social situation, another one-quarter of the expectancies dealt with drinking to gain control of a situation. Interestingly, in a recent report by Blume et al., (2006), it was concluded that cognitions about drinking may not only predict consumption patterns, but also may predict the experience of negative drinking consequences. According to the authors, a significant portion of recent consequences experienced by individuals were not necessarily related to drinking per se, but rather were related to cognitions; for instance, the expected effects of alcohol and the self-efficacy for successfully negotiating high-risk situations without drinking heavily.

Data reduction only allows preliminary results regarding the Lesch alcoholism classification in heroin dependent patients, in what observes a tendency in type IV patients to present a high severity profile regarding the cognitive and behavioral dimensions assessed. This tendency is congruent with a high severity subgroup as Lesch type IV patients (Pombo and Lesch, 2009).

In the study we should consider some limitations: Like in other studies, our data demonstrate a high prevalence of drinking problems among patients undergoing opiate maintenance treatment. However, comparisons across studies should be done cautiously, since diverse study methods have used different instruments to assess alcohol use and abuse, producing some heterogeneity in the results prevalence's. In the study we did not measure other psychological dimensions that could account for the differences in the

IDTS profiles. In some extent, other possible explanation accounting for the differences in IDTS profiles between type I and type II patients could be the notion of motivation to change (Prochaska and DiClemente, 1986). Indeed, studies have argued that readiness to change account for the differentiation of IDTS drinking profiles, with more motivated people reporting higher overall IDTS scores or greater differentiation of IDTS subscales and least motivated showing low totals scores and undifferentiated profiles (Annis and Graham; 1995; Turner et al., 1997). As Turner et al. (1997) states, patients with lack of awareness of their drinking (pre-contemplation stage) would have little interest, and maybe little awareness of how their affective states and external circumstances influenced their alcohol use; on the other hand, patients that have made a decision to change (determination stage), would have paid more attention on their alcohol use patterns. Moreover, addiction denial could also provide another plausible interpretation for the differences in IDTS in the subtypes. Alcohol abuse denial defines the notion of the drinker refusal to acknowledge his pathological alcohol use or minimizing the relation between alcohol consumption and his psychological, organic and social problems. In psychodynamic terms, denial is usually considered as an unconscious ego defense mechanism. Other authors propose that alcoholic denial is more related to cognitive failure than an ego defense mechanism, consisting in a diminished capacity for insight, for example, due to executive function failure (Rinn et al., 2002). A recent study performed in alcoholic patients have demonstrated that Cloninger's type II patients reported lower levels of alcoholism denial, when compared with type I patients (Pombo et al., 2008a). Indeed, since type I patients tend to become more defensive regarding alcohol use it will be expected that they tend to refuse or turn hesitant in identifying their real high-risk situations, and as result, a lower and more undifferentiated IDTS profile could emerge. In the psychometric study of IDTS performed by Turner et al., (1997), other dimensions were found to influence IDTS scores. For example, the authors concluded that individuals who reported that they spend little time using unaccompanied and experience pressure from family or friends to use substances, had higher scores on the IDTS interpersonal subscales of PT and SP, while individuals who assumed spending more time using substances alone had elevations on the IDTS intrapersonal subscales of UE and PD.

We also may found some inconsistencies regarding the alcohol related expectancies in this population, since this association may vary by population heterogeneity, polysubstance use and levels and time-course of substance use.

The screening for drug metabolites in urine analyses, a procedure that incorporates the clinical routine of our addiction unit, was properly controlled by the nurse staff. Nevertheless, alcohol use was only assessed by patients self-reports providing a possible reliability limitation in the interview, given the fact that participants with an excessive alcohol use may tend to underestimate or deny alcohol consumption and related problems. Therefore, a more accurate determination of patient alcohol consumption levels, for example, urine analyses or liver function, should be performed. For example, Stenbacka et al., (2007), posits that most studies on MMT patients consider the alcohol use information based on records from interviews and questionnaires, and only occasionally using laboratory tests. Indeed, a recent study of the authors found a significant association between the number of alcohol-related diagnoses prior to treatment and a positive 5HTOL/5HIAA (sensitive biomarker of acute alcohol consumption) test during MMT.

It's also important to bring up some technical issues applying the Lesch classification procedure to opiate dependent patients who meet also the criteria for alcohol dependence, since items related to alcohol withdrawal or seizures could also be attached to a frequent behavior in this population like higher levels of benzodiazepine use.

Finally, we should also consider limitations due to the relatively small sample size of the study, the heterogeneity of the population and the fact that gender differences were not examined due to small cell sizes. So, it's not clear without further evaluation that these data could be generalized to other populations of drinkers.

Conclusion

A range of different factors that differ from person to person influences aetiology and outcomes of addiction. In research and clinical practice, the evaluation of different functions such as screening, assessment, diagnosis, treatment planning and follow-up, are an essential step to identify behaviors and associated problems and to improve prevention and treatment in a population that often seeks help related to the misuse of substances (Hester and Miller, 2003).

Studies have been assembling empirical evidence for the treatment of alcohol dependence in general (Johnson and Ait-Daoud, 2000; Hester and Miller, 2003; Saitz, 2007), particularly relapse prevention pharmaceutical agents such as naltrexone and acamprosate. In the meantime, when we extend the clinical management of an alcohol problem to methadone-using patients, we may face several boundaries in the treatment outcome, mostly related to the complexity inherent to polysubstance use, abuse or dependence and also because we must consider the exception of a pharmacologically effective tool in the treatment of alcoholism such as naltrexone since it is contraindicated in methadone-using patients.

A more accurate clinical establishment of the nature of the relationship between alcohol and opioids, would be useful in planning treatment for opioid dependent patients with concurrent alcohol use, with particular focus on relapse prevention not only for heroin use but for other drugs and alcohol as well (Stenbacka et al., 2007; Srivastava et al., 2008).

The study concluded that in general, heroin-dependent patients classified as type II problem drinkers demonstrate a more severe alcohol-taking profile than those with a type I alcohol problem. Nevertheless, upon closer examination we were be able to identify different situation-specific prototypes of alcohol use, in which heroin-dependent patients classified as type II problem drinkers were much more vulnerable to negative situation triggers like intrapsychic unpleasant emotions or interpersonal confliction, than heroin-dependent patients classified as type I problem drinkers. These high-risk situations in type II patients, along with more positive beliefs and expectancies about alcohol effect may increase the chance for ineffective coping responses with an unremitting alcohol abuse pattern. Therefore, these cognitive-behavioral indicators should help the clinician to better tailor the intervention in this particular population. Indeed, treatment outcomes may be further improved if clinical subtypes of substance abusers could be identified and matched to an adequate treatment. Given this potential impact, evidence comes from the observation that type A alcoholics have better outcomes in interactional treatment and do more poorly with coping skills training and in opposition, type B alcoholics had better outcomes with the coping skills treatment and worse outcomes with interactional therapy (Litt et al., 1992). To some extent, these findings from Litt et al. (1992) may have clinical implications in our study, since type A patients from Babor et al. (1992) and type I from Cloninger et al. (1981) are in some way similar (low-severity/vulnerability subgroup), as Babor et al. (1992) type B and Cloninger et al. (1981) type II (high-severity/vulnerability subgroup).

With a cognitive-behavioral multidimensional assessment of relevant indicators such as alcohol craving, type and degree of beliefs and expectations related to alcohol effects and the identification of taxonomic high-risk situations for alcohol use would enable the substance abuse psychological health-care to focus on the management of specific areas to prevent problem drinking and reduce current harm associated with their lifestyle. Indeed, the cognitive-behavioral measurement and conceptualization underlying the pathological drinking in heroin dependence is essential in the development of successful psychoeducational messages and relapse prevention strategies related to alcohol use. Cognitive-behavioral therapists should teach patients a broad range of coping skills to avoid or deal with the return of previous excessive alcohol use, such as problem solving, challenging distorted thoughts, relaxation, assertiveness, modeling and functional analysis. In cases following an assessment of specific alcohol-use functions reported by patients with polysubstance use pattern, the mental health clinicians, in interaction with patients, should encourage them to indentify high-risk situations in as much detail as possible and develop alternative ways of fulfilling these functions. Nevertheless, it is imperative to posit that these psychological strategies only succeed with patients if therapists always keep up efforts to build a good therapeutic relationship with them. For example, Dundon et al., (2008), focused on a factor that is common to all types of psychosocial treatments for substance abuse—the therapeutic alliance between the patient and the clinician. According to the authors, the therapeutic alliance reflects the nature and strength of the affective bond between patient and primary clinician in their collaboration in identifying and working toward the patient's treatment goals.

Future investigations need to be considered in order to continuously update the cognitive-behavioral background with new empirical findings about clinical subgroups and polysubstance abuse life courses.

REFERENCES

Agrawal, S., Sobell, M. B., & Sobell, L. C. (2007). The Timeline Followback: A scientifically and clinically useful tool for assessing substance use. In R. F. Belli, F. P. Stafford, & D. F. Alwin (Eds.), *Using calendar and diary methodologies in life events research.* Beverly Hills, CA: Sage Publications.

Allen, J. P. and Wilson, V. B. (2003) *Assessing alcohol problems: A guide for clinicians and researchers.* National Institute of Alcohol Abuse and Alcoholism, Bethesda.

Almog YJ, Anglin MD, Fisher DG. (1993) Alcohol and heroin use patterns of narcotics addicts: gender and ethnic differences. *Am. J. Drug Alcohol Abuse;* 19:219–38.

Amaro H, Mangual S, Nieves RL.(2004a) Spirituality in recovery: *An educational group curriculum for women in recovery.* Boston Consortium of Services for Families in Recovery, Public Health Commission, Boston, MA.

Amaro H, Nieves RL, Saunders L. (2004b) Women's Leadership Training Institute: *An educational group curriculum for women in recovery.* Boston Consortium of Services for Families in Recovery, Public Health Commission, Boston, MA.

Ambrose ML, Bowden SC, Whelan G (2001). Working memory impairments in alcohol-dependent participants without clinical amnesia. *Alcoholism: Clinical and Experimental Research;* vol.25, No.2, pp 185-191.

Andersohn, F. & Kiefer, F. (2004). Depressive mood and craving during alcohol withdrawal: association and interaction. *German Journal Psychiatry,* 7, 6-11.

Anglin, M. D., Almog, I. J., Fisher, D. G., & Peters, K. R. (1989). Alcohol use by heroin addicts: Evidence for an inverse relationship. A study of methadone maintenance and drug-free treatment samples. *American Journal of Drug and Alcohol Abuse*. 15, 191– 207.

Annis, H. M., & Graham, J. M. (1995). Profile types on the Inventory of Drinking Situations: Implications for relapse prevention counselling. *Psychology of Addictive Behaviours*. 9, 176-182.

Annis, H.M. & Martin, G. (1985). Inventory of Drug-Taking Situations. Toronto, Canada: Addiction Research Foundation.

Arasteh, K., Des Jarlais, D.C., Perlis, T. (2008). Alcohol and HIV sexual risk behaviors among injection drug users. *Drug Alcohol Depend*. 95, 54–61.

Avants SK, Warburton LA, Margolin A. (2001) Spiritual and religious support in recovery from addiction among HIV-positive injection drug users. *Journal of Psychoactive Drugs;* 33(1): 39–46.

Babor & Caetano (2006) Subtypes of substance dependence and abuse: implications for diagnostic classification and empirical research. *Addiction*. 101(sup):104-110.

Babor, T. F., De Hofmann, M. I., Boca, F. K., Hesselbrock, V., Meyer, R. E., Dolinsky, Z. S. & Rounsaville, B. (1992) Types of alcoholics, I: evidence for an empirically derived typology based on indicator of vulnerability and severity. *Archives of General Psychiatry*. 49, 599-608.

Babor, T.F., Biddle-Higgins, J.C., Saunders, J.B. & Monteiro, M.G. (2001). AUDIT: The Alcohol Use Disorders Identification Test: Guidelines for Use in Primary Health Care. Geneva, Switzerland: World Health Organization.

Backmund M, Schutz CG, Meyer K, Eichenlaub D, Soyka M. (2003) Alcohol consumption in heroin users, methadone-substituted and codeine-substituted patients-frequency and correlates of use. *Eur. Addict. Res;* 9:45–50.

Baetz M, Bowen R, Jones G, Koru-Sengul T.(2006) How spiritual values and worship attendance relate to psychiatric disorders in the Canadian population. *Canadian Journal of Psychiatry;* (51): 654–661.

Ball S. A. Carroll K. M. ; Babor T. F ; Rounsaville B. (1995) Subtypes of cocaine abusers: support for a Type A-Type B distinction. *Journal of Consulting and Clinical Psychology*. 63, 115-124.

Bandura, A. (1977) Self-efficacy: toward a unifying theory of behavioural change. *Psychological Review*. 84, 191–215.

Barrett ME, Simpson D, Lehman WE.(1988) Behavioral changes of adolescents in drug abuse intervention programs. *Journal of Clinical Psychology;* 44: 461–473.

Bartzokis G, Beckson M, Lu PH et al. Age-related brain volume reductions in amphetamine and cocaine addicts and normal controls: implications for addiction research. *Psychiatry Res.* 2000; 98:93_102.

Beck A, Wright F, Newman C, Liesh B. (1993) *Cognitive Therapy of Substance Abuse.* New York: Guilford Press.

Bellis, M., Hughes, K., Bennett, A. and Thomson, R. (2003), 'The role of an international nightlife resort in the proliferation of recreational drugs', *Addiction,* 98, pp. 1713–21.

Bergeret J. (1983) Toxicomania e personalidade, Rio de Janeiro, Zahar Ed.

Bertschy, G. (1995). Methadone maintenance treatment: An update. *European Archives of Psychiatry and Clinical Neuroscience.* 245, 114–125.

Best, D., Gossop, M., Lehmann, P., Harris, J., & Strang, J. (1999). The relationship between overdose and alcohol consumption among methadone maintenance patients. *Journal of Substance Use.* 4, 41– 44.

Beswick, T., Best, D., Rees, S., Coomber, R., Gossop, M., Strang, J., (2001). Multiple drug use: patterns and practices of heroin and crack use in a population of opiate addicts in treatment. *Drug Alcohol. Rev.* 20, 201–204.

Bleich S, Bayerlein K, Reulbach U, Hillemacher T, Bönsch D, Mugele B, Kornhuber J, Sperling W. (2004) Homocysteine levels in patients classified according to Lesch's typology. *Alcohol and Alcoholism.* 39(6), 493-498.

Blum RW, Halcón L, Beuhring T, Pate E, Campell-Forrester S, Venema A. (2003) Adolescent health in the Caribbean: risk and protective factors. *American Journal of Public Health;* 93(3): 456–460.

Blume AW, Lostutter T, Schmaling K, Marlatt A. (2003) Beliefs about drinking behavior predict drinking consequences, *Journal of Psychoactive Drugs.* 35(3), 395–399.

Bolla KI, Ernst M, Kiehl KA, Mouratidis M, Eldreth DA et al (2004) Prefrontal cortical dysfunction in abstinent cocaine abusers. *J. Neuropsych. Clin.* N 16:456–464.

Bolla KI, Rothman R, Cadet JL. Dose-related neurobehavioral effects of chronic cocaine use. *J. Neuropsychiatry Clin. Neurosci.* 1999; 11:361_369.

Booth B, Leukefeld C, Falck R, Wang J, Carlson R, (2006). Correlates of rural methamphetamine and cocaine users: results from a multistate community study. *J. Stud. Alcohol.* 67, 493–501.

Bovasso, G., Cacciola, J. (2003). The long-term outcomes of drug use by methadone maintenance patients. *J. Behav. Health Serv. Res.* 30, 290–303.

Boys, A., Fountain, J., Marsden, J. et al. (1999), 'What influences young people's use of drugs? *A qualitative study of decision-making', Drugs: Education, Prevention and Policy.* 6, pp. 373–89.

Breslin, F. C., Sobell, L. C., Sobell, M. B., & Agrawal, S. (2000). A comparison of a brief and long version of the Situational Confidence Questionnaire. *Behaviour Research and Therapy.* 38, 1211-1220

Brewer DD, Catalano RF, Haggerty K, Gainey RR, Fleming CB.(1998) A meta-analysis of predictors of continued drug use during and after treatment for opiate addiction. *Addiction;* 93: 73–92.

Brown BS, O'Grady KE, Farrell EV, Fechner IS, Nurco DN.(2001) Factors associated with frequency of 12-step attendance by drug abuse clients. *American Journal of Drug and Alcohol Abuse;* 27: 147–160.

Brown SA, Carrello PD, Vik PW, Porter RJ. (1998) Change in alcohol effect and self-efficacy expectancies during addiction treatment. *Substance Abuse;* 19:155–67.

Brown SA, Christiansen BA, Goldman MS (1987). The Alcohol Expectancy Questionnaire: an instrument for the assessment of adolescent and adult alcohol expectancies. *J. Stud. Alcohol.* Sep; 48(5):483-91.

Brown SA, Goldman MS, Christiansen BA. (1985) Do alcohol expectancies mediate drinking patterns of adults? *Journal of Consulting and Clinical Psychology.* 53, 512-19.

Brown, S. A., Goldman, M. S., Inn, A. et al. (1980) Expectations of reinforcement from alcohol: Their domain and relation to drinking patterns. *Journal of Consulting and Clinical Psychology.* 48, 419–426.

Byqvist, S., (2006). Patterns of drug use among drug misusers in Sweden gender differences. *Subst. Use Misuse.* 41, 1817–1835.

Caputo F, Addolorato G, Domenicali M,_Mosti A, Viaggi M, Trevisani F, Gasbarrini G, Bernardi M and Stefanini G , & The Services For Addiction Treatment (2002) Short-term methadone administration reduces alcohol consumption in non-alcoholic heroin addicts. *Alcohol Alcohol.* 37, 164 – 16 8.

Cardoso, J.M., Barbosa, A., Ismail, F. and Pombo, S. (2006) Neter Alcoholic Typology (NAT). *Alcohol and Alcoholism.* 41, 133-139.

Carpenter KM, Hasin DS (2001) Reliability and discriminant validity of the type I/II and type A/B alcoholic subtype classifications in untreated problem drinkers: a test of the Apollonian-Dionysian hypothesis. *Drug and Alcohol Dependence.* 63, 51-67.

Chatham, L. R., Rowan-Szal, G. A., Joe, G. W., Brown, B. S., & Simpson, D. D. (1995). Heavy drinking in a population of methadone-maintained clients. *Journal of Studies on Alcohol.* 7, 417– 422.

Ciccocioppo R., Antonelli L., Biondini M., Perfumi M., Pompei P., Massi M. (2002) Memory impairment following combined exposure to delta(9)-tetrahydrocannabinol and ethanol in rats. *European Journal of Pharmacology;* 449:245-251.

Cloninger, C. R., Bohman, M. & Sigvardsson, S (1981). Inheritance alcohol abuse: cross fostering analysis of adopted men. *Archives of General Psychiatry.* 38, 861868.

Colzato L, Huizinga M & B Hommel. (2009) Recreational cocaine polydrug use impairs cognitive flexibility but not working memory. *Psychopharmacology;* 207:225–234.

Connors G J; O'Farrell T J; Pelcovits M A. (1988). Drinking outcome expectancies among male alcoholics during relapse situations. *British journal of addiction.* 83(5), 561-6.

Cooney, N.L., Litt, M.D., Morse, P.A., Bauer, L.O. & Gaupp, L. (1997). Alcohol cue reactivity, negative mood reactivity, and relapse in treated alcoholics men. *Journal Abnormal Psychology.* 106, 243-250.

Costa NF, Pombo S, Barbosa F. (2008) A propósito da avaliação clínica numa consulta de toxicodependências *Toxicodependências.* 14, 25-34.

Cunningham JA. (2000) Remissions from drug dependence: Is treatment a prerequisite? *Drug and Alcohol Dependence;* 59: 211–213.

D'Aunno, T., & Vaughn, T. E. (1992). Variations in methadone treatment practices. Results from a national study. *Journal of the American Medical Association.* 267, 253– 258.

Dafters R, Hoshi R, Talbot A (2004). Contribution of cannabis and MDMA ("ecstasy") to cognitive changes in long-term polydrug users. *Psychopharmacology;* 173:405–410.

Darke S, Sims J, McDonald S, Wickes W (2000) Cognitive impairment among methadone maintenance patients. *Addiction;* 95:687, 695.

Darke, S., Ross, J., Teesson, M. (2007). The Australian Treatment Outcome Study ATOS: what have we learnt about treatment for heroin dependence? Drug Alcohol. Rev. 26, 49–54.

Dawes MA, Antelman SM, Vanyukov MM, Giancola P, Tarter RE, Susman EJ, et al.(2000) Developmental sources of variation in liability to adolescent substance use disorders. *Drug and Alcohol Dependence;* 61(1): 3–14.

Demir B, Ulug B, Lay E, Erbas B (2002). Regional cerebral blood flow and neuropsychological functioning in early and late onset alcoholism. *Psychiatric Research;* 1:115(3):115-25.

Dermatis H, Guschwan MT, Galanter M, Bunt G. (2004) Orientation toward spirituality and self-help approaches in the therapeutic community. *Journal of Addictive Diseases;* 23(1).

DiClemente, C.C. & Hughes, S.O. (1990). Stages of change profiles in alcoholism treatment. *Journal of Substance Abuse,* 2, 217-235.

Dobler-Mikola, A., Hattenschwiler, J., Meili, D., Beck, T., Boni, E., Modestin, J. (2005). Patterns of heroin, cocaine, and alcohol abuse during long-term methadone maintenance treatment. *J. Subst. Abuse Treat.* 29, 259–265.

Downey, K., Helmus, T., Schuster, C. (2000). Treatment of heroin-dependent poly-drug abusers with contingency management and buprenorphine maintenance. *Exp. Clin. Psychopharmacol.* 8, 176–184.

Duka T, Townshend JM, Collier K, Stephens DN (2003) Impairment in cognitive functions after multiple detoxifications in alcoholic inpatients. *Alcoholism: Clinical and Experimental Research;* Vol.27, No10, pp 1563-1572.

Dundon W, Pettinati H, Lynch K, Xie H, Varillo K, Makadon C, Oslin D. (2008) The therapeutic alliance in medical-based interventions impatcs outcome in treating alcohol dependence. *Drug and Alcohol Dependence* 95, 230–236.

Dvorak A, Pombo S, Ismail F, Barbosa A, Cardoso JM, Figueira ML, Walter H, Lesch OM (2006). Tipologias da dependência do álcool e o seu significado para a terapêutica médica. *Acta Psiquiátrica Portuguesa* 52, 1693-1705.

Edwards G, Gross MM (1976). Alcohol dependence: provisional description of a clinical syndrome. Br. Med. J. May 1;1058–1061

El-Bassel, N., Schilling, R. F., Turnbull, J. E., & Su, K.-H. (1993). Correlates of alcohol use among methadone patients. *Alcoholism: Clinical and Experimental Research.* 17, 681– 686.

El-Bassell N, Schilling RF. (1992) 15 month follow-up of women methadone patients taught skills to reduce heterosexual HIV transmission. *Public Health Reports;* 107: 500–504.

Eldreth DA, Matochik JA, Cadet JL, Bolla KI (2004) Abnormal brain activity in prefrontal brain regions in abstinent marijuana users. *Neuroimage;* 23:914:920.

Ellison CG. (1991) Religious involvement and subjective well-being. *Journal of Health and Social Behavior;* 32(1): 80–99.

EMCDDA (2007), Selected issue, Drugs and driving, European Monitoring Centre for Drugs and Drug Addiction, Lisbon.

EMCDDA (2009), Polydrug use: patterns and responses. European Monitoring Centre for Drugs and Drug Addiction, Lisbon.

Ersche KD, Fletcher PC, Lewis SJ et al. (2005) Abnormal frontal activations related to decision-making in current and former amphetamine and opiate dependent individuals. *Psychopharmacology;* 180:612_623.

Everitt B. (1997) Craving cocaine cues: cognitive neuroscience meets drug addiction research. *Trends Cogn. Sci.* (Regul. Ed.); 1: 1.

Ewing JA (1984) Detecting alcoholism. The CAGE questionnaire. *JAMA;* 252(14):1905-7.

Fairbank, J.A., Dunteman, G.H., & Condelli, W.S. (1993). Do methadone patients substitute other drugs for heroin? Predicting substance use at 1-year follow-up. *American Journal of Drug and Alcohol Abuse.* 19, 465–474.

Fein G, Di Sclafani V, Meyerhoff DJ (2002) Prefrontal cortical volume reduction associated with frontal cortex function deficit in 6-week abstinent crack-cocaine dependent men. *Drug Alcohol Depend*; 68:87:93.

Feng Y, Xun SS, Wang XH. (1999) Study on depression and anxiety of 50 cases heroin reliers before and after detoxification therapy. *Chinese Journal of Drug Abuse Prevention and Treatment;* 18(1): 12-15.

Fingarette H. (1988) Heavy Drinking: The Myth of Alcoholism as a Disease. Berkeley, CA: University of California Press.

Finn PR, Sharkansky EJ, Brandt KM, Turcotte N. (2000). The effects of familial risk, personality, and expectancies on alcohol use and abuse. *Journal of Abnormal Psychology.* 109:122–133.

Finney JW, Monahan SC. (1996) The cost effectiveness of treatment for alcoholism: A second approximation. *Journal of Studies on Alcohol;* 57: 229-243.

Fishbein DH; Krupitsky E; Flannery BA; Langevin DJ; Bobashev G; Verbitskaya E; Augustine CB; Bolla KI; Zvartau E; Schech B; Egorova V; Bushara N; Tsoy M. (2007) Neurocognitive characterizations of Russian heroin addicts without a significant history of other drug use. *Drug Alcohol Depend;* 90(1):25-38.

Flannery, B., Morgenstern, J., McKay, J., Wechsberg, W., Litten, R. (2004). Cooccurring alcohol and cocaine dependence: recent findings from clinical and field studies. *Alcohol Clin. Exp. Res.* 28, 976–981.

Flannery, B.A., Volpicelli, J.R. & Pettinati. (1999). Psychometric properties of the Penn Alcohol Craving Scale. *Alcoholism: Clinical Experimental Research*. 8, 1289-1295.

Gelb, A. M., Richman, B. L., & Anand, O. P. (1978). Quantitative and temporal relationships of alcohol use in narcotic addicts and methadone maintenance patients undergoing alcohol detoxification. *American Journal of Drug and Alcohol Abuse*. 5, 191–198.

Gitto S., Micco L., Conti F., Andreone P. and Bernardi M. Alcohol and viral hepatitis: A mini-review : *Dig. Liver Dis.* 2009 Jan;41(1):67-70.

Goeders NE. (2003) The impact of stress on addiction. *European Neuropsychopharmacology,* 13: 435–441.

Gonzalez R, Rippeth JD, Carey CL et al. (2004) Neurocognitive performance of methamphetamine users discordant for history of marijuana exposure. *Drug Alcohol Depend;* 76:181:190.

Goodwin D.W.; Crane J.B, Guze S.B. (1969) Phenomenological aspects of the alcoholic "blackout." *British Journal of Psychiatry;* 115:1033-1038.

Goodwin, D.W.; Schulsinger, F.; Hermansen, L.; Guze, S.B.; & Winokur, G. (1973) Alcohol problems in adoptees raised apart from alcoholic biological parents. *Archives of General Psychiatry*. 28:238-243.

Gossop M, Marsden J, Stewart D, Kidd T. (2003) The National Treatment Outcome Research Study (NTORS): 4–5 year follow-up results. *Addiction*; 98: 291–303.

Gossop M, Marsden J, Stewart D. (2002a) Dual dependence: assessment of dependence upon alcohol and illicit drugs, and the relationship of alcohol dependence among drug misusers to patterns of drinking, illicit drug use and health problems. *Addiction*. 97:169–78.

Gossop M, Stewart D, Marsden J. (2006) Effectiveness of drug and alcohol counselling during methadone treatment: content, frequency, and duration of counselling and association with substance use outcomes. *Addiction*. 101, 404–12.

Gossop, M. (1996). Cognitive and behavioural treatments for substance misuse. In Edwards G. & Dare C. (Ed.), *Psychotherapy, Psychological Treatments and the Addictions* (158-172). Great Britain. Cambridge University Press.

Gossop, M. (2001). A web of dependence. *Addiction*. 96, 677–678.

Gossop, M., Marsden, J., Stewart, D. et al. (1998), 'Substance use, health and social problems of clients at 54 drug treatment agencies: intake data from the National Treatment Outcome Research Study (NTORS)', *British Journal of Psychiatry*. 173, pp. 166–71.

Gossop, M., Marsden, J., Stewart, D., & Rolfe, A. (2000). Patterns of improvement after methadone treatment: 1 year follow-up results from the National Treatment Outcome Research Study. *Drug and Alcohol Dependence.* 60, 275–286.

Gossop, M., Marsden, J., Stewart, D., Kidd, T. (2002b). Changes in use of crack cocaine after drug misuse treatment: 4–5 year follow-up results from the National Treatment Outcome Research Study NTORS. *Drug Alcohol Depend.* 66, 21–28.

Gossop, M., Stewart, D., Browne, N., & Marsden, J. (2003). Methadone treatment for opiate dependent patients in general practice and specialist clinic settings: Outcomes at 2-year follow-up. *Journal of Substance Abuse Treatment.* 24, 313– 321.

Granfield R, Cloud W. (1999) Coming clean: Overcoming addiction without treatment. New York: New York University Press.

Grant I, Judd LL (1976) Neuropsychological and EEG disturbances in polydrug users. *Am. J. Psychiatry.* Sep; 133(9):1039-42.Green, J., & Jaffe, J. H. (1977). Alcohol and opiate dependence; a review. *Journal of Studies on Alcohol.* 38, 1274– 1293.

Guerra D, Sole A, Cami J, Tobena A. (1987) Neuropsychological performance in opiate addicts after rapid detoxification. *Drug Alcohol Depend;* 20:261:270.

Haaga DAF, McCrady B, Lebow J. (2006) Integrative Principles for Treating Substance Use Disorders. *Journal of Clinical Psychology;* 62 (6): 675–684.

Harper C, Matsumoto I. Ethanol and brain damage. *Current opinion in Pharmacology.* 2005; 5:73-78.

Hartel, D. M., Schoenbaum, E. E., Selwyn, P. A., Kline, J., Davenny, K., Klein, R. S., et al. (1995). Heroin use during methadone maintenance treatment: The importance of methadone dose and cocaine use. *American Journal of Public Health.* 85, 83– 88.

Hartzler B, Fromme K. (2003) Fragmentary blackouts: Their etiology and effect on alcohol expectancies. *Alcoholism: Clinical and Experimental Research.* Vol.27, No.4: 628-637.

Hester R, Garavan H (2004) Executive dysfunction in cocaine addiction: evidence for discordant frontal, cingulate, and cerebellar activity. *J. Neurosci.* 24:11017–11022

Hester R. K. & Miller W.R. (2003). *Handbook of Alcoholism Treatment Approaches.* USA. Pearson Education Inc..

Hillebrand, J., Marsden, J., Finch, E., & Strang, J. (2001). Excessive alcohol consumption and drinking expectations among clients in methadone maintenance. *Journal of Substance Abuse Treatment.* 21, 155–160.

Hillemacher T, Bayerlein K, Wilhelm J, Bönsch D, Poleo D, Sperling W, Kornhuber J, Bleich S. (2006) Recurrent detoxifications are associated with craving in patients classified as type I according to Lesch's typology. *Alcohol and Alcoholism.* 41(1), 66-69.

Hillemacher, T. and Bleich, S. (2008) Neurobiology and treatment in alcoholism--recent findings regarding Lesch's typology of alcohol dependence. *Alcohol and Alcoholism.* 43, 341-6.

Hodge DR, Cardenas P, Montoya H. (2001) Substance use: spirituality and religious participation as protective factors among rural youths. *Social Work Research,* 25(3): 153–160.

Hser YI, Hoffman V, Grella CE, Anglin MD. (2001) A 33-year follow-up of narcotics addicts. *Arch. Gen. Psychiatry.* 58, 503 – 8.

Hser, Y. I., Anglin, M. D., & Powers, K. (1990). Longitudinal patterns of alcohol use by narcotics addicts. *Recent Developments in Alcoholism.* 8,145– 171.

Hubbard, R., Craddock, S., Flynn, P., Anderson, J., Etheridge, R., (1997). Overview of 1 year follow-up outcomes in the Drug Abuse Treatment Outcome Study DATOS. *Psychol. Addict. Behav.* 11, 261–278.

Hunt, D.E., Strug, D.L., Goldsmith, D.S., Lipton, D.S., Robertson, K., & Truitt, L. (1986). Alcohol use and abuse: Heavy drinking among methadone clients. *American Journal of Drug and Alcohol Abuse.* 12, 147–164.

Ives, R. and Ghelani, P. (2006), 'Polydrug use (the use of drugs in combination): a brief review', *Drugs: Education, Prevention and Policy,* 13, pp. 225–32.

Jellinek EM. Phases in the drinking history of alcholics: analysis of a survey conducted by the official organ of Alcoholics Anonymous. *Q. J. Stud. Alcohol.* 1946; (7), 1-88.

Jiang ZN, Wang WP. (1992) Drug abuse. Beijing: *Technology Publishing Company,* 119-209.

John, D., Kwiatkowski, C., Booth, R. (2001). Differences among out-of-treatment drug injectors who use stimulants only, opiates only or both: implications for treatment entry. *Drug Alcohol Depend.* 64, 165–172.

Johnson BA, Ait-Daoud N. (2000) Neuropharmacological treatments for alcoholism: scientific basis and clinical findings. *Psychopharmacology.* 149, 327–44.

Jones, B. T. and McMahon, J. (1992) Negative and positive expectancies in lone and group problem drinkers. *British Journal of Addiction.* 87, 929–930.

Joseph H, Appel P. (1985) Alcoholism and methadone treatment: consequences for the patient and program. *Am. J. Drug Alcohol Abuse.* 11:37–53.

Kabat-Zinn J, Chapman A, Salmon P. (1997) The relationship of cognitive and somatic components of anxiety to patient preference for alternative relaxation techniques. *Mind/Body Medicine;* 2: 101–109.

Kabat-Zinn, J. (1982) An outpatient program in behavioral medicine for chronic pain patients based on the practice of mindfulness meditation: Theoretical considerations and preliminary results. *General Hospital Psychiatry;* 4: 33–47.

Kaplan MS, Marks G, et al. (1997) Distress and coping among women with HIV infection: Preliminary findings from a multiethnic sample. *American Journal of Orthopsychiatry;* 67(1): 80–91.

Kaufman, E. (1982). The relationship of alcoholism and alcohol abuse to the abuse of other drugs. *American Journal of Drug and Alcohol Abuse.* 9, 1–17.

Kelly GA. (1955) The Psychology of Personal Constructs. New York: Norton.

Kendler KS, Gardner CO, et al. (1997) Religion, psychopathology, and substance use and abuse: A multimeasure, genetic-epidemiologic study. *American Journal of Psychiatry;* 154(3): 322–329.

Khantzian EJ, Halliday KS, McAuliffe WE. (1990) Addiction and the vulnerable self. New York: Guilford Press.

Khantzian EJ. (1980) An ego-self theory of substance dependence. In Lettieri DJ, Sayers M. & Wallensterin HW (eds), Theories of addiction. NIDA Research Monograph No. 30 DHHS Publication No. ADM 80-967. Washington DC: Superintendent of Documents, U.S. Government Printing Office, 1980.

Khantzian EJ. (1985) The self-medication hypothesis of addictive disorders: Focus on heroin and cocaine dependence. Am J Psychiatry;142: 1259-64.

Kokavec A, Crowe S.(1999) A comparison of cognitive performance in binge versus regular chronic alcohol misusers. *Alcohol and Alcoholism;* Vol.24, pp.601-608.

Kosten TR, Rounsaville BJ, Kleber HD. (1986) A 2.5 year follow-up of depressions, life crises, and treatment effects on abstinence among opioid addicts. *Archives of General Psychiatry,* 43: 733–739.

Kreek MJ. (1978) Medical complications between opiates and alcohol. *Ann. N.Y. Acad. Sci.* 362, 36 – 49.

Kreek, M. J. (1984). Opioid interactions with alcohol. *Advances in Alcohol & Substance Abuse*. 3, 35–46.

Kreek, M.J. (1990). Drug interactions in humans related to drug abuse and its treatment. *Modern Methods in Pharmacology*. 6, 265–282.

Krupitsky E, Burakov A, Romanova T, Dunaevsky I, Strassman R, Grinenko A. (2002) Ketamine psychotherapy for heroin addiction: immediate effects and two-year follow-up. *Journal of Substance Abuse Treatment;* 23: 273–283.

Laudet AB, Morgen K, White WL. (2006) The role of social supports, spirituality, religiousness, life meaning and affiliation with 12-step fellowships in quality of life satisfaction among individuals in recovery from alcohol and drug problems. *Alcohol Treatment Quarterly;* 24(1–2): 33–73.

Leri, F., Bruneau, J., Stewart, J. (2003). Understanding polydrug use: review of heroin and cocaine co-use. *Addiction.* 98, 7–22.

Lesch O, Riegler A, Gutierrez K, Hertling I, Ramskogler K, Semler B, Zoghlami A, Benda N, Walter H (2001). The European Acamprosate Trials: conclusions for research and therapy. *J. Biomed. Sci.* 8, 89-95.

Lesch, O. M., Dietzel, M., Musalek, M., Walter, H. and Zeiler, K (1988). The course of alcoholism. Long-term prognosis in different Types. *Forensic Science International.* 36, 121–138.

Liang JH, Ren YH. (2001) The study on drug abuse's addicted mechanism, epidemiology, prevention and cure. *Chinese Journal of Drug Depend;* 10(1): 2-8.

Litt MD, Babor TF, DelBoca FK, Kadden RM and Cooney NL (1992) Types of alcoholics: II. Application of an empirically derived typology of treatment matching, *Archives of General Psychiatry.* 49, 609–614.

Litt, M.D., Cooney, N.L. & Morse, P. (2000). Reactivity to alcohol-related stimuli in the laboratory and in the field: predictors of craving in treated alcoholics. *Addiction.* 95, 889-900.

Lotfi J, Meyer JS.(1989) Cerebral hemodynamic and metabolic effects of chronic alcoholism. *Cerebrovasc Brain Metabolism Rev;* 1:2-25.

Lowman, R., Allen, J., Stout, R. L., & Relapse Research Group (1996). Marlatt's taxonomy of relapse precipitants: Overview of procedures and results. *Addiction*. 91, 51–72.

Lykouras L, Moussas G, Botsis (2004) Examination of type I/II alcoholism typology in a Greek hospital treatment population. *European Psychiatry* 19, 214-218.

Lyoo IK, Pollack MH, Silveri MM et al. (2006) Prefrontal and temporal gray matter density decreases in opiate dependence. *Psychopharmacology;* 184:139:144.

Maddux, J. F., & Elliot, B. (1975). Problem drinkers among patients on methadone. *American Journal of Alcohol Abuse.* 2, 245– 254.

Magura, S., Nwakeze, P.C.& Demsky S.Y. (1998). Preditors of Treatment Retention in Methadone Treatment. *Addiction.* 93, 51-60.

Malcolm, B., Hesselbrock, M., Segal, B. (2006). Multiple substance dependence and course of alcoholism among Alaska native men and women. *Subst. Use Misuse.* 51, 729–741.

Mann K, Agartz I, Shoaf S, Momenam R, Hommer DW, Sullivan EV, Drobes DJ, George MK, Bares R, Mundle G, Heinz A (2001). Neuroimaging in alcoholism: ethanol and brain damage. *Alcoholism: Clinical and Experimental Research;* Vol. 25, No5, pp 104-109.

Maremmani, I., Pani, P.P., Mellini, A., Pacini, M., Marini, G., Lovrecic, M., Perugi, G., Shinderman, M., (2007). Alcohol and cocaine use and abuse among opioid addicts engaged in a methadone maintenance treatment program. *J. Addict. Dis.* 26 (1), 61–70.

Margolin A, Beitel M, Schuman-Olivier Z, Avants SK. (2006) A controlled study of a spirituality-focused intervention for increasing motivation for HIV prevention among drug users. *AIDS Education & Prevention;* 18(4): 311–322.

Marlatt GA, Witkiewitz K, Dillworth TM, Bowen SW, Parks GA, Macpherson LM. (2004) Vipassana meditation as a treatment for alcohol and drug use disorders. In S. C. Hayes, V. M. Follette, & M. M. Linehanm (Eds.), *Mindfulness and acceptance: Expanding the cognitive-behavioral tradition* (pp. 261–287). New York: Guilford Press.

Marlatt, G. A. & Gordon, J. R. (Eds.) (1985). Relapse prevention: Maintenance strategies in the treatment of addiction behaviour. New York: Guilford Press

Marlatt, G. A. & Roseenow, D. J. (1980) Cognitive processses in alcohol use: expectancy and the alanced placebo design, in: N. K. Mello (Ed.) *Advances in Substance Abuse: behavioral and biological research.* 1, 159-199 (Greenwich, CT, JAI Press)

Marsden J, Eastwood B, Bradbury C, Dale-Perera A, Farrell M, et al. (2009) Effectiveness of community treatments for heroin and crack cocaine addiction in England: a prospective, in-treatment cohort study. *Lancet;* 374: 1262–70.

Martin, C. S., Clifford, P. R., Maisto, S. A. Earleywine M, Kirlsci L, Longabaugh R. (1996) Polydrug use in an inpatient treatment sample of problem drinkers. *Alcoholism: Clinical and Experimental Research.* 20, 413–417.

Mattick, R. P., Breen, C., Kimber, J., & Davoli, M. (2003). Methadone maintenance therapy versus no opioid replacement therapy for opioid dependence. *Cochrane Database of Systematic,* 2.

Maxwell, S., & Shinderman, M. (1999). Optimizing response to methadone maintenance treatment: Use of higher-dose methadone. *Journal of Psychoactive Drugs*. 31, 95– 102.

McLellan AT, Grissom GR, Zanis D, Randall M, Brill P, O'Brien CP. (1997) Problemservice 'matching' in addiction treatment. A prospective study in 4 programs. *Archives of General Psychiatry;* 54: 730–735.

McLellan, A.T., Luborsky, L., O'Brien, C.P. & Woody, G.E. (1980). An improved diagnostic instrument for substance abuse patients: The Addiction Severity Index. *Journal of Nervous & Mental Diseases,* 168, 26-33.

Medina, K., Shear, P. (2007). Anxiety, depression, and behavioural symptoms of executive dysfunction in ecstasy users: contributions of polydrug use. *Drug Alcohol Depend.* 87, 303–311.

Melgaard B, Henriksen L, Ahlgren P, Danielsen UT, Sorensen H, Paulson OB. (1993) Regional cerebral blood flow in chronic alcoholics measured by single photon emission on computerized tomography. *Acta Neurologica Scandinavica;* 82, 87-93.

Miller JJ, Fletcher K, Kabat-Zinn J. (1995) Three-year follow-up and clinical implications of a mindfulness meditation-based stress reduction intervention in the treatment of anxiety disorders. *General Hospital Psychiatry;* 17: 192–200.

Miller L, Davies M, Greenwald S. (2000) Religiosity and substance use and abuse among adolescents in the national comorbidity survey. *Journal of the American Academy of Child and Adolescent Psychiatry;* 39(9): 1190–1197.

Miller WR, Brown SA. (1997) Why psychologists should treat alcohol and drug problems. *American Psychologist;* 52: 1269-1279.

Miller WR, Zweben A, DiClemente CC, Rychtarik RG. (1992) Motivational enhancement therapy manual: a clinical research guide for therapists treating individuals with alcohol abuse and dependence (Vol. 2, Project

MATCH Monograph Series). Rockville, MD: National Institute on Alcohol Abuse and Alcoholism.

Miller WR. (1998) Researching the spiritual dimensions of alcohol and other drug problems. Addiction; 93: 979–990.

Miller, W. R., & Tonigan, J. S. (1996). Assessing drinkers' motivation for change: The Stages of Change Readiness and Treatment Eagerness Scale (SOCRATES). *Psychology of Addictive Behaviors,* 10, 81–89.

Miller, W.R., Tonigan, J.S. & Longabaugh, R. (1995). The Drinker Inventory of Consequences (DrInC): An Instrument for Assessing Adverse Consequences of Alcohol Abuse. Project MATCH Monograph Series, Vol. 4. DHHS Publication No. 95-3911. Rockville, MD: National Institute on Alcohol Abuse and Alcoholism.

Modell, J.G., Glaser, F.B., Mountz, J.M., Schmaltz S. & Cyr, L. (1992). Obsessive and compulsive characteristics of alcohol abuse and dependence: Quantification by a newly developed questionnaire. *Alcoholism: Clinical Experimental Research,* 16, 266-271.

Molina JA, Bermejo F, del Ser T, Jimenez-Jimenez FJ, Herranz A, Fernandez-Calle P, Ortuno B, Sainz MJ. (1994) Alcoholic cognitive deterioration and nutritional deficiencies. *Acta Neurologia Scandinavica;* 89, 384-390.

Moos RH. (2003) Addictive disorders in context: Principles and puzzles of effective treatment and recovery. *Psychology of Addictive Behaviors;* 17: 3–12.

Moos, R (2005). Iatrogenic effects of psychosocial interventions for substance use disorders: prevalence, predictors, prevention. *Addiction.* 100, 595 – 604.

Morel A, Hervé F, Fontaine B. (1998) Abordagens Psicológicas. In Morel A, Hervé F, Fontaine B (eds) *Cuidados ao toxicodependente.* Lisboa: Climepsi Editores.

Morgenstern J, Leeds J. (1993) Contemporary psychoanalytic theories of substance abuse: A disorder in search of a paradigm. *Psychotherapy;* 30: 194-206.

National Institute on Alcohol Abuse and Alcoholism (1995). The Physician's Guide to Helping Patients with Alcohol Problems. US DHHS NIH Publ. No. 95-3769. Washington, DC: PHS.

National Treatment Agency for Substance Misuse. (2006) Models of care for adult drug misusers: update. http://www.nta.nhs.uk/ publications/ documents/nta_modelsofcare_update_2006_moc3.pdf

Nava F, Manzato E, Leonardi C, Lucchini A. (2008) Opioid maintenance therapy suppresses alcohol intake in heroin addicts with alcohol dependence: Preliminary results of an open randomized study. *Progress in Neuro-Psychopharmacology & Biological Psychiatry* 32, 1867–1872.

Neff JA, Shorkey CT, Windsor LC. (2006) Contrasting faith-based and traditional substance abuse treatment programs. *Journal of Substance Abuse Treatment;* 30: 49–61.

Nelson EC, Heath AC, Bucholz KK, Madden PA, Fu Q, Knopik V, Lynskey MT, Whitfield JB, Statham DJ, Martin NG (2004). Genetic epidemiology of alcohol-induced blackouts. *Archives of General Psychiatry.* Vol.61, pp. 257-263.

O'Grady, K., Arria, A., Fitzelle, D. & Wish, E. (2008), 'Heavy Drinking and Polydrug Use among College Students', *Journal of Drug Issues*, 38(2), pp. 445-466.

O´Leary MR, Donovan DM, Chaney EF. (1979) Cognitive impairment and treatment outcome in alcoholics: preliminary findings. *Journal of Clinical Psychiatry;* 40, 397-398.

O'Mahony, J. (2004) A Comparison of Alcohol Abusers who have and have not Experienced Blackouts. *European Addiction Research;* 10(3): pp. 95-98.Oei TPS, Baldwin AR (1994) Expectancy theory: A two-process model of alcohol use and abuse. *Journal of Studies on Alcohol.* 55, 525-534.

Oei TPS, Fergusson S, Lee NK. (1998) The differential role of alcohol expectancies and drinking refusal self efficacy in problem and nonproblem drinkers. *Journal of Studies on Alcohol.* 59, 704–11.

Olievenstein C. (1982) A Vida do Toxicómano. Rio de Janeiro: Zahar.

Olivenstein C. (1987) La Dependence: Un Phénomène Psychique Actif in Olivenstrein C, Angel P, Géraud B, Mège JY, Perpére A, Petit P, Valleur M. La Clinique du Toxicomane, Paris, Editions Universitaires, p. 13-24.

Oorsouw KV, Merckelbach H, Ravelli D, Nijman H, Mekking-Pompen I.(2004) Alcoholic blackout for criminally relevant behavior. *The Journal of the American Academy of Psychiatry and the Law;* 32, pp. 364-70.

Ornstein TJ, Iddon JL, Baldacchino AM et al. (2000) Profiles of cognitive dysfunction in chronic amphetamine and heroin abusers. *Neuropsychopharmacology;* 23:113:126.

Oscar-Berman M, Kirkley SM, Gansler DA, Couture A.(2004) Comparisons of Korsakoff and non-Korsakoff alcoholics on neuropsychological tests of prefrontal brain functioning. *Alcohol: Clinical and Experimental Research;* 28(4):667-75.

Ottomanelli G. (1999) Methadone patients and alcohol abuse. *J. Subst. Abuse Treat.* 16, 113–21.

Ottomanelli, G. (1992). HIV infection and intravenous drug use. Westport, CT: Praeger

Pagès-Berthier J. (2002) Personalidade e toxicomania: abordagem psicanalítica. *In* Angel P, Richard D, & Valleur M. (Eds.). *Toxicomanias* (pp. 179-185). Lisboa: Climepsi Editores.

Pandey, G.N., Fawcett, J., Gibbons, R., Clark, D.C., David, J.M. (1988) Platelet monoamine oxidase in alcoholism. *Biological Psychiatry*. 24, 15-24.

Pardini DA, Plante TG, et al. (2000) Religious faith and spirituality in substance abuse recovery: Determining the mental health benefits. *Journal of Substance Abuse Treatment;* 19(4): 347–354.

Patterson, T., Semple, S., Zians, J., Strathdee, S. (2005). Methamphetamineusing HIV-positive men who have sex with men: correlates of polydrug use. *J. Urban Health.* 82 (Suppl. 1), 120–126.

Pau CW, Lee TM, Chan SF. (2002) The impact of heroin on frontal executive functions. *Arch. Clin. Neuropsychol;* 17:663: 670.

Pessione F, Gerchstein JL, Rueff B. (1995) Parental history of alcoholism: a risk factor for alcohol related peripheral neuropathies. *Alcohol and Alcoholism;* 30, 749-754.

Pinto Gouveia, J., Ramalheira, C., Robalo, M., Borges, J. Almeida; J. (1993). Inventário de expectativas e crenças pessoais acerca do álcool. *Psiquiatria Clínica 14*, 147-163.

Poikolainen K.(1982) Blackouts increase with age, social class and the frequency of intoxication. *Acta Neurol. Scand;* 66, 555-560.

Pombo S, Lesch OM. (2009) The alcoholic phenotypes among different multidimensional typologies: similarities and their classification procedures. *Alcohol Alcohol.* 44, 46-54

Pombo, S., Ismail, F. & Neves Cardoso. J,M. "Cravers" pelo álcool. *Revista Psicologia, Saúde & Doenças* (in press)

Pombo, S., Levy, P., Bicho, M., Ismail, F., Cardoso, J.M.(2008b) Neuropsychological function and platelet monoamine oxidase activity levels in type I alcoholic patients. *Alcohol Alcohol.* 43, 423–30.

Pombo, S., Reizinho, R., Ismail, F. & Neves Cardoso. J,M, (2008a). Denegação do alcoolismo nos subtipos I e II de Cloninger. *Análise Psicológica,* XXVI, 59-69.

Pombo, S., Reizinho, R., Ismail, F., Barbosa, A., Luísa Figueira, M., Neves Cardoso, J.M., Lesch, O.M. (2007). NETER Alcoholic 5 Subtypes: Validity with Lesch 4 Evolutionary Subtypes. *International Journal of Psychiatry in Clinical Practice,* 1-10.

Pope HG Jr, Gruber AJ, Hudson JI, Cohane G, Huestis MA, Yurgelun-Todd D.(2003) Early-onset cannabis use and cognitive deficits: what is the nature of the association? D*rug Alcohol Depend;* 69:303:310.

Prescott, C.A., and Kendler, K.S (1999). Genetic and environmental contributions to alcohol abuse and dependence in a population–based sample of male twins. *American Journal of Psychiatry*. 156: 34–40.

Prochaska, J.O. & DiClemente, C.C. (1986). Toward a comprehensive model of change. In W. Miller and N. Heather (Eds.), Addictive behaviours: Processes of Change. New York: Plenum Press, 3-28.

Rado S. (1933) The psychoanalysis of pharmacotymias. *Psychoanal Q*; 2:1-23.

Rask MB, Jørgensen T, Jensen JP, Jørgensen KB, Madsen M, Nielsen B, et al. (2006) Influence of Pretreatment Coping Strategies on the Outcome of Outpatient Treatment of Danish Alcohol Abusers. *European Addiction Research;* 12: 83–90.

Ratti MT, Soragna D, Sibilla L, Giardini A, Albergati A, Savoldi F, Bo P. (1999) Cognitive impairment and cerebral atrophy in "heavy drinkers". *Neuro-psychopharmacology and biology psychiatry;* vol.23, pp- 243-258.

Rinn W, Desai N, Rosenblatt H, Gastfriend DR (2002). Addiction denial and cognitive dysfunction: a preliminary investigation. *J. Neuropsychiatry Clin Neuroscience.* 14, 52-57.

Rittmannsberger H, Silberbauer C, Lehner R, Ruschak M. (2000) Alcohol consumption during methadone maintenance treatment. *Eur. Addict. Res.* 6:2–7.

Rodríguez M.(1993) Cognitive functioning in male polydrug abusers with and without family history of alcoholism. *Percept Mot. Skills.* Oct;77(2):483-8.

Roehrich L and Goldman MS. (1993) Experience-dependent neuropsychological recovery and the treatment of alcoholism. *J. Cons. Clin. Psychology;* (5), 812-21.

Rollnick, S., Heather, N., Gold, R. and Hall, W. (1992) Development of a short 'readiness to change' questionnaire for use in brief, opportunistic interventions among excessive drinkers. *British Journal of Addiction* 87, 743–754.

Room R, Babor T, Rehm J (2005). Alcohol and public health. *Lancet,* 365:519–529

Rosa A. (1994) Toxicodependência: as desintoxicações ultra-rápidas. Coimbra: [s.n], 94(2).

Roszell, D. K., Calsyn, D. A., & Chaney, E. F. (1986). Alcohol use and psychopathology in opioid addicts on methadone maintenance. *American Journal of Drug and Alcohol Abuse* 12, 269– 278.

Rounsaville, B.J., Weissman, M.M., & Kleber, H.D. (1982). The significance of alcoholism in treated opiate addicts. *Journal of Nervous and Mental Disease* 170, 479–488.

Rourke SB, Loberg T. (1996) Neurobiological correlates of alcoholism. In Grant I, Adams KM. Neuropsychological assessment of neuropsychiatric disorders; New York, USM, Oxford University Press.

Rowan-Szal, G. A., Chatham, L. R., & Simpson, D. D. (2000). Importance of identifying cocaine and alcohol dependent methadone clients. *American Journal on Addictions* 9, 38–50.

Rubonis, A.V., Colby, S.M., Monti, P.M., Rosenow, D.J., Gulliver, S.B. & Sirota, A.D. (1994). Alcohol cue reactivity and mood induction in male and female alcoholics. *Journal Studies Alcohol.* 55, 487-494.

Ryback RS.(1970) Alcohol amnesia: observations in seven drinking inpatient alcoholics. *Q. J. Stud. Alcohol;* 31, 616-632.

Saitz, Richard (2007). Treatment of Alcohol and Other Drug Dependence. *Liver Transplantation.* 13, 59-64.

Schiff, E. R. (1997). Hepatitis C and alcohol. *Hepatology*. 26, 39S– 42S.

Schottenfeld, R. S., Pakes, J. R., & Kosten, T. R. (1998). Prognostic factors in buprenorphine- versus methadone-maintained patients. *Journal of Nervous and Mental Disease*. 186, 35– 43.

Schut, J., File, K., & Wohlmuth, T. (1973). Alcohol use by narcotic addicts in methadone maintenance treatment. *Quarterly Journal of Studies on Alcohol*. 34, 1356– 1359.

Selzer M.L. (1971). The Michigan Alcoholism Screening Test (MAST): the quest for a new diagnostic instrument. *American Journal Psychiatry.* 127, 1653– 1658.

Senbanjo R, Wolff K, Marshall J. (2006) Excessive alcohol consumption is associated with reduced quality of life among methadone patients. *Addiction;* 102:257–63.

Serra A.V., Lima M.M. (1979). O uso do «Michigan Alcoholism Screening Test» como instrumento discriminador entre grupos de alcoólicos e de não-alcoólicos. *Coimbra Médica.* 197, 39-5.

Silvers JM, Tokunaga S, Berry RB, White AM, Mattews DB. (2003) Impairments in spatial learning and memory: ethanol, allopregnanolone, and the hippocampus. *Brain Research Reviews;* 43, 275-284.

Simpson D., George J. & Grace A. (1997). Drug Abuse Treatment Retention and Process Effects on Follow-up Outcomes. *Drug and Alcohol Dependence,* 47, 227-235.

Sinha R, Fuse T, Aubin LR, O'Malley SS. (2000) Psychological stress, drug-related cues, and cocaine craving. *Psychopharmacology;* 152: 140–148.

Skinner H (1982) The Drug Abuse Screening Test. *Addictive Behaviors.* 7:363–371

Sklar S. M; Annis H. M.; Turner N. E. (1997) Development and validation of the Drug-Taking Confidence Questionnaire: A measure of coping self-efficacy. *Addictive behaviors.* 22, 655-670.

Sobell, L. C., & Sobell, M. B. (2003). Alcohol consumption measures. In J. P. Allen & V. Wilson (Eds.), Assessing alcohol problems (2nd ed.) (pp. 75-99). Rockville, MD: National Institute on Alcohol Abuse and Alcoholism.

Solowij N, Stephens RS, Roffman RA et al. (2002) Cognitive functioning of long-term heavy cannabis users seeking treatment. *JAMA;* 287:1123:1131.

Southwick, L., Steele, C., Marlatt, G. A., & Lindell, M. (1981). Alcohol-related expectancies: Defined by phase of intoxication and drinking experience. *Journal of Consulting and Clinical Psychology,* 49, 713-721.

Soyka M, Zingg C, Koller G, Kuefner H. (2008) Retention rate and substance use in methadone and buprenorphine maintenance therapy and predictors of outcome: results. *Int. J. Neuropsychopharmacol.* 21, 1-13.

Srivastava, A., Kahan, M., Ross, S. (2008). The effect of methadone maintenance treatment on alcohol consumption: a systematic review. *J. Subst. Abuse Treat.* 34, 215–223.

Stacy AW, Widaman KF, Marlatt GA. (1990) Expectancy models of alcohol use. *Journal of Personality and Social Psychology.* 58:918–928.

Staines, G. L., Magura, S., Foote, J. et al. (2001) Polysubstance use among alcoholics. *Journal of Addictive Diseases.* 20, 53–69.

Stein MD, Cioe P, Friedmann PD. (2005) Buprenorphine retention in primary care. *J. Gen. Intern. Med.* 20(11), 1038-41.

Stenbacka, M., Beck, O., Leifman, A., Romelsjo, A., Helander, A. (2007). Problem drinking in relation to treatment outcome among opiate addicts in methadone maintenance treatment. *Drug Alcohol Rev*. 26, 55–63.

Stevens A, Peschk I, Schwarz J. (2007) Implicit learning, executive function and hedonic activity in chronic polydrug abusers, currently abstinent polydrug abusers and controls. *Addiction*. Jun;102(6):937-46.

Stimmel, B., Vernace, S., & Tobias, H. (1972). Hepatic dysfunction in heroin addicts. The role of alcohol. *Journal of the American Medical Association.* 222, 811 – 812.

Strang, J., Griffiths, P., & Powis, B. (1999). Fountain, J., Williamson, S., & Gossop, M. (1999) Which drugs cause overdose among opiate misusers? Study of personal and witnessed overdoses. *Drug and Alcohol Review.* 18, 253– 261.

Strang, J., Marsden, J., Cummins, M., Farrell, M., Finch, E., Gossop, M., Stewart D, Welch S. (2000). Randomized trial of supervised injectable versus oral methadone maintenance: Report of feasibility and 6-month outcome. *Addiction.* 95, 1631– 1645.

Sullivan EV, Fama R, Pferfferbaum M. (2002) A profile of neuropsychological deficits in alcoholic women. *Neuropsychology;* Vol.16, No.1, pp. 74-83.

Sullivan EV, Rosenbloom MJ, Pfefferbaum A. (2000) Pattern of cognitive and motor deficits in detoxified alcoholic men. *Alcoholism: Clinical and Experimental Research.* 2000, 24:611-621.

Sullivan, J.L., Baenziger, J.C., Wagner, D.L. (1990) Platelet MAO in subtypes of alcoholism. *Biological Psychiatry.* 27, 911-922.

Sumnall, H., Wagstaff, G., Cole, J. (2004). Self-reported psychopathology in polydrug users. J. *Psychopharmacol.* 18, 75–82.

Tarter, RE, Schneider DU. (1976) Blackouts: Relationship with memory capacity and alcoholism history. *Arch. Gen. Psychiatry;* 33:1492-1496.

Taylor PJ, Kopelman MD.(1984) Amnesia for criminal offenses. *Psychol. Med;* 14, 581-8.

Teplin, D., Raz, B., Daiter, J., Varenbut, M., Plater-Zyberk, C. (2007). Screening for alcohol use patterns among methadone maintenance patients. *Am. J. Drug Alcohol Abuse.* 33, 179–183.

Toates F. (1998) The interaction of cognitive and stimulus – response processes in the control of behaviour. *Neurosci. Biobehav. Rev*; 22: 59–83.

Turner, N. E., Annis, H. M., & Sklar, S. M. (1997). Measurement of Antecedents to Drug and Alcohol Use: Psychometric Properties of the Inventory of Drug-Taking Situations (IDTS). *Behav. Res. Ther.* 35, N. 5.

Verkes RJ, Gijsman HJ, Pieters MSM, Schoemaker RC, de Visser S, Kuijpers M, Pennings EJM, de Bruin D, Van de Wijngaart G, Van Gerven JMA, Cohen AF (2001) Cognitive performance and serotonergic function in users of ecstasy. *Psychopharmacology.* 153:196–202.

Volkow ND, Fowler JS, Wang GJ (1999) Imaging studies on the role of dopamine in cocaine reinforcement and addiction in humans. J. *Psychopharmacol.* 13:337–345 von Knorring, A. L., Bohman, M., von Knorring, L. and Oreland, L. (1985) Platelet MAO activity as a biological marker in subgroups of alcoholism. *Acta Psychiatrica Scandinavica.* 72, 51–58.

von Knorring, A.L., Hallman, J., von Knorring, L., Oreland, L. (1998) Platelet monoamine oxidase activity in type 1 and type 2 alcoholism. *Alcoholism: Clinical and Experimental Research.* 22, 598-604.

Waldrop A, Back S, Verduin M, Brady K. (2007).Triggers for cocaine and alcohol use in the presence and absence of posttraumatic. *Addictive behaviors*. 32, 634-9.

Walter H; Ramskogler-Skala K; Dvorak A; Gutierrez-Lobos K; Hartl D; Hertling I; Munda P; Thau K; Lesch O; Witte P (2006) Glutamic acid in withdrawal and weaning in patients classified according to Cloninger´s and Lesch´s typologies. *Alcohol & Alcoholism* 41, 505-511.

Waltman D. (1995) Key Ingredients to Effective Addictions Treatment. *Journal of Substance Abuse Treatment;* 12 (6): 429-439.

Weaver GD, Turner NH, O'Dell KJ. (2000) Depressive symptoms, stress, and coping among women recovering from addiction. *Journal of Substance Abuse Treatment;* 18: 161–167.

West, S L, O'Neal, K K, Graham, C W. (2000) A meta-analysis comparing the effectiveness of buprenorphine and methadone. *J-Subst-Abuse*. 12(4), 405-14.

Westreich LM. (2005) Alcohol and mental illness: clinical focus. *Prim. Psychiatry*. 12:41–6.

White AM, Jamieson-Drake D, Swartzwelder HS. (2002) Prevalence and correlates of alcohol-induced blackouts among college students: Results of an e-mail survey. *J. Am. College Health;* 51,117-131.

White AM, Signer ML, Kraus CL, Swartzwelder HS. (2004) Experimental aspects of alcohol-induced blackouts among college students. *The American Journal of Drug and Alcohol Abuse;* Vol.30, No.1, pp. 205-224.

White AM, Simson PE, Best PJ.(1997) Comparison between the effects of ethanol and diazepam on spatial working memory in the rat. *Psychopharmacology;* 133:256-261.

White, W, Kurtz, E. (2006) The varieties of recovery experience. *International Journal of Self Help and Self Care,* 2006; 3: 21−61.

Williamson, A., Darke, S., Ross, J., Teesson, M., (2006). The effect of persistence of cocaine use on 12-month outcomes for the treatment of heroin dependence. *Drug Alcohol Depend.* 81, 293–300.

Windle, M. and Scheit, D. M. (2004) Alcoholic subtypes: are two sufficient? *Addiction.* 99, 1508–1519.

Witkiewitz K, Marlatt GA, Walker DD. (2005) Mindfulnessbased relapse prevention for alcohol use disorders: The meditative tortoise wins the race. *Journal of Cognitive Psychotherapy;* 19: 211–230.

World Health Organization (2004).Global status report: alcohol policy. Geneva.

World Health Organization, WHO (1994). International Statistical Classification of Diseases and Related Health Problems. Tenth Revision. Geneva: WHO.

Wurmser L. (1985) Denial and split identity: timely issues in the psychoanalytic psychotherapy of compulsive drug users. *Journal of Substance Abuse Treatment;* 2: 89-96.

Wurmser L. (1987) Flight from conscience: experiences with the psychoanalytic treatment of compulsive drug abusers. *Journal of Substance Abuse Treatment;* 4: 169-179.

Yan YM, Xu H , Li DY. (2000) Questionnaire analysis on physical-mental health state in 169 cases heroin addicts. *Guizhou Medical Journal;* 24 (5): 318.

Yan YQ, Liu YY, Zeng YF, Cui YW, Lei JW, Wang ZZ. (2008) Evaluation of Effectiveness of Integrated Intervention Program in Improving Drug Addicts' Psychological Health. *Biomedical and Environmental Sciences;* 21: 75-84.

Young, R. M., & Knight, R. G. (1989). The Drinking Expectancy Questionnaire: A revised measure of alcohol-related beliefs. *Journal of Psychopathology and Behavioral Assessment.* 11, 99−112.

Young, R. McD., Oei, T.P.S. & Crook, C.M. (1991). Development of a Drinking Self Efficacy Scale. *Journal of Psychopathology and Behavioral Assessment,* 13(1), 1-15.

Yücel M; Lubman D; Solowij N; Brewer W. (2009) Understanding drug addiction: a neuropsychological perspective. *Australian and New Zealand Journal of Psychiatry,* 41:12,957 — 968.

Zador S, Sunjic D. (2000) Deaths in methadone maintenance treatment in New South Wales, Australia, 1990–1995. *Addiction.* 95:77–86.

Zinn S, Stein R, Swartzwelder S. (2004) Executive functioning early in abstinence from alcohol. *Alcoholism: Clinical and Experimental Research;* Vol.28; No 9, pp 1338-1346.

INDEX

A

B

D

E

O

P

Q

R

T

U

V

W

Y